The
Doberman
Pinscher

An Owner's Guide To

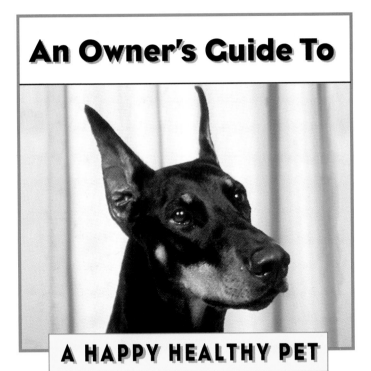

A HAPPY HEALTHY PET

Howell Book House

Howell Book House

A Simon & Schuster Macmillan Company
1633 Broadway
New York, NY 10019

Library of Congress Cataloging-in-Publication Data
Beauchamp, Richard G.
The Doberman pinscher : an owner's guide to happy, healthy pet / Rick Beauchamp.
p. cm.

ISBN: 0-87605-481-5

1. Doberman pinschers. I. Title.
SF429.D6B424 1996
636.7'3—dc20   96-6040
                    CIP

Manufactured in the United States of America
10 9 8 7 6 5 4 3 2 1

Series Director: Dominique De Vito
Series Assistant Directors: Ariel Cannon and Sarah Storey
Book Design: Michele Laseau
Cover Design: Iris Jeromnimon
Illustration: Jeff Yesh
Photography:
  Cover Photos by Paulette Braun/Pets by Paulette. Back Cover photo by Gay Glazbrook.
  Joan Balzarini: 96
  Richard Beauchamp: 23, 52
  Mary Bloom: 96, 136, 145
  Paulette Braun/Pets by Paulette: 11, 46, 56, 62, 64, 92, 96
  Buckinghamhill American Cocker Spaniels: 148
  Sian Cox: 134
  Dr. Ian Dunbar: 98, 101, 103, 111, 116–117, 122, 123, 127
  Gay Glazbrook: 9, 25, 35
  Dan Lyons: 96
  Scott McKiernan/Zuma: 15, 31, 50, 54, 72, 134
  Cathy Merrithew: 129
  Liz Palika: 133
  Cheryl Primeau: 27, 30, 65
  Susan Rezy: 5, 82, 96–97, 136, 145
  Judith Strom: 6, 13, 22, 58, 68, 96, 107, 110, 128, 130, 135, 137, 139, 140, 144, 149, 150
  Jean Wentworth: 29, 32, 40, 42, 78
  Karrin Winter: 49, 63, 66, 67
Production Team: Trudy Brown, Jama Carter, Kathleen Caulfield, Trudy Coler, Amy DeAngelis, Matt Hannafin, Vic Peterson, Terri Sheehan and Marvin Van Tiem

Contents

Welcome
to the
World
of the

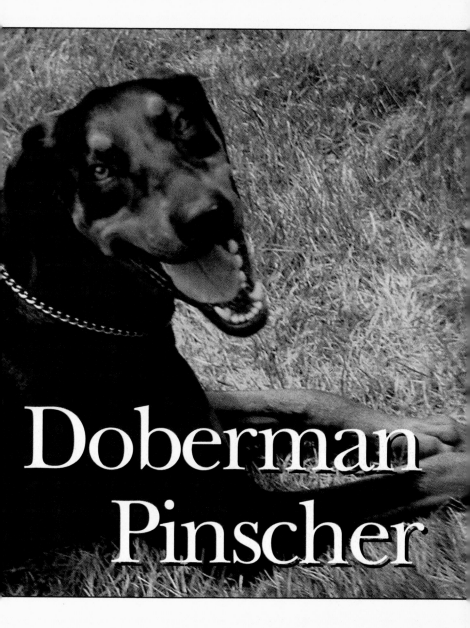

part one

Doberman Pinscher

External Features of the Doberman Pinscher

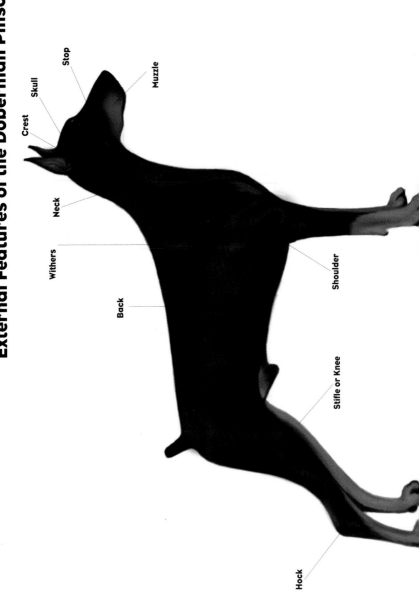

chapter 1

What
Is a
Doberman
Pinscher?

The well-bred Doberman Pinscher is without a doubt one of the most honest breeds of dog known to man. What you see is indeed what you get. There is nothing superfluous in the properly conditioned Doberman's appearance. There is nothing hidden or camouflaged by a long or cleverly trimmed coat. There are no pendulous ears or scimitar tail; nothing extraneous under the close-fitting jacket.

A Dignified Dog

If you observe a hint of arrogance and aloofness in the mature Doberman, you are spot on in your evaluation. There is nothing fawning or slavish in the character of the dog blessed with true Doberman Pinscher temperament.

Devotion, yes, but never subservience. In a word, this is a breed of great dignity and integrity.

The Doberman's devotion manifests itself in an inherent desire to protect those he loves and the territory in which they reside. The Doberman is a marvelous watch dog, a versatile companion and undoubtedly one of the most receptive and trainable members of the canine world.

While this is indeed true of the mature Doberman, the Doberman youngster can be as bouncy, as clumsy and as inept as a puppy of any other breed. There is one difference, however, that I have observed in the Doberman puppy which sets him apart from the youngsters of most other breeds. While the Doberman is as guilty of adolescent ineptness as any breed, this ineptness seems a cause of embarrassment to even the most scattered youngster.

The head of the Doberman reflects the breed's sleek lines.

Quilla, our first Doberman, arrived at our home as an eight-week-old puppy on one of the first truly warm days of spring. Looking to enjoy an afternoon sun bath, Quilla found an outdoor sling chair—canvas hung on a wire frame. Her little body cradled itself neatly in the seat of the chair. Each day, after exhausting herself with the many things the young Doberman finds to do, she would seek out "her chair" for that afternoon siesta.

As the days and weeks rolled by and the metamorphosis from a roly-poly baby to all-legs teenager took place, Quilla found it increasingly more difficult to fit into her treasured place in the sun. She would look at the chair in amazement and do her utmost to ease herself into the space that had held her easily and comfortably for so many weeks. After a time, the sling chair was simply too small to hold her at all. The contortions that

Quilla put herself through to get comfortable in the chair that no longer accommodated her at all would send us all into gales of laughter. Our enjoyment of her predicament continued until one day Quilla stopped in the midst of her futile attempts and looked at us. It was as if she realized we were laughing at her. That day was the last Quilla attempted to use "her chair."

The Breed Standard

(For a complete copy of the Doberman Pinscher Standard, contact the Doberman Pinscher Club of America. Address on page 37.)

The nobility, power and grace which characterize the Doberman Pinscher are reflected in the official standard of the breed as written by the Doberman Pinscher Club of America. This written depiction of the breed is intended to serve as a guide so that the qualities of appearance and character which make this breed unique are maintained.

Responsible breeders strive to maintain these characteristics in each and every breeding they make. These breeders are well aware of the many variables which make achieving the perfect dog an impossible dream. The responsible know, however, that while perfection is elusive, those qualities which make the Doberman such a highly respected breed must never be neglected.

First and foremost, the Doberman is a compact dog of "medium" size which in essence is a requirement aimed at keeping the breed in a manageable size range—a size allowing a person of average stature to easily reach down while standing erect and keep their hand on the dog's collar. Not too big, not to small—simply a size compatible with easy control.

> ### WHAT IS A BREED STANDARD?
>
> A breed standard—a detailed description of an individual breed—is meant to portray the *ideal* specimen of that breed. This includes ideal structure, temperament, gait, type—all aspects of the dog. Because the standard describes an ideal specimen, it isn't based on any particular dog. It is a concept against which judges compare actual dogs and breeders strive to produce dogs. At a dog show, the dog that wins is the one that comes closest, in the judge's opinion, to the standard for its breed. Breed standards are written by the breed parent clubs, the national organizations formed to oversee the well-being of the breed. They are voted on and approved by the members of the parent clubs.

In the following discussion of the Doberman Pinscher Standard, the official standard is given in italics, and the author's commentary appears below it.

HEIGHT

The appearance is that of a dog of medium size, with a body that is square; the height, measured vertically from the ground to the highest point of the withers, equaling the length measured horizontally from the forechest to the rear projection of the upper thigh.

Measurements for all breeds of dogs are obtained by measuring the distance from the withers, which is the top-most point of the shoulders, to the ground. In Dobermans the ideal measurement at this point is about twenty-seven-and-one-half inches for males and about twenty-five-and-one-half inches for females. Dobermans of this size have the imposing but elegant look so important to the breed. A Doberman of the size described is big enough to make the average intruder think twice, but not so large as to be difficult for the owner to control.

SHYNESS AND VICIOUSNESS

The judge shall dismiss from the ring any shy or vicious Doberman.

While temperament will be dealt with in greater detail in Chapter 3, it is critical to understand that shyness or viciousness are unforgivable faults in the Doberman Pinscher. Poor temperament should never be tolerated under any circumstances. Correct temperament characterizes the ideal Doberman more than any other single attribute. The breed standard could not be more specific or emphatic in its demands regarding temperament and it bears repeating here.

HEAD

Long and dry resembling a blunt wedge in both frontal and profile views. When seen from the front the head widens gradually toward the base of the ears in a practically unbroken line. Top of skull flat turning with slight stop to bridge of muzzle, with muzzle line extending parallel to top line of skull.

The head of a given breed of dog does most to truly identify the breed and assists greatly in defining the breed's character. If this is so, the head of the Doberman Pinscher does indeed reflect the breed's sleek lines and elegant structure. Never coarse or heavy in appearance, the ideal Doberman's head is clean of line while still maintaining a sense of strength and power. It is moderately long, and the top of the skull is flat and parallel to the line of the muzzle.

Eyes *Almond shaped, moderately deep set, with vigorous, energetic expression.*

The dark and unobtrusive eyes of the Doberman create an expression that spells intelligence, awareness and courage. A large, light-colored or yellow eye gives a wild and fearful look which totally alters the desired expression of the breed.

Teeth *Strongly developed and white . . . a true scissors bite.*

Working dogs like the Doberman Pinscher, as well as the many Herding breeds, use their mouths in the work that they do. Therefore, a full compliment of strongly developed, white teeth is impor-
tant. The "scissors bite" called for in the Doberman standard is one in which the outer surfaces of the lower front teeth engage with the inner surfaces of the upper front teeth when the mouth is closed. It is said that the jaw constructed to accommodate the scissors bite is capable of inflicting the most punishing bite of all.

Historically the Doberman's ears have been cropped, but this is up to the owner.

The Doberman was developed as a guard dog capable of dispatching intruders. In order for any breed to function in this capacity, he does with his mouth what a human being would do with his or her hands. For this reason the construction of the jaws and placement of the teeth in the Doberman are extremely important.

Of the four disqualifications listed in the standard of the breed, three relate to faults found in the breed's jaws and mouth. A breed standard "disqualification" is a fault so serious that a dog may not be shown in American Kennel Club dog shows. Most breeders agree that a dog who has a disqualifying fault as listed in the breed standard should never be bred. Doing so would only serve to perpetuate the extreme fault.

Ears   *Normally cropped and carried erect.*

Historically the Doberman's ears have been cropped. There are several good reasons for this. From a strictly utilitarian sense, the cropped ear gave adversaries, whether human or canine, less to grab hold of in a confrontation. Hygienically, the ear canal open to air circulation is far less susceptible to infections and accumulation of wax or moisture. Cosmetically the cropped, high set, pointed ear gives the Doberman the alert, intelligent look which is a hallmark of the breed.

There is allowance made for the uncropped ear in the American breed standard which describes the ears as "*normally* cropped and carried erect." (Italics mine.) The decision to crop or not to crop remains with the individual owner if this has not been done before the purchase is made. Still, if a show career is in the offing for one's Doberman, the uncropped dog would stand with a

THE AMERICAN KENNEL CLUB

Familiarly referred to as "the AKC," the American Kennel Club is a nonprofit organization devoted to the advancement of purebred dogs. The AKC maintains a registry of recognized breeds and adopts and enforces rules for dog events including shows, obedience trials, field trials, hunting tests, lure coursing, herding, earthdog trials, agility and the Canine Good Citizen program. It is a club of clubs, established in 1884 and composed, today, of over 500 autonomous dog clubs throughout the United States. Each club is represented by a delegate; the delegates make up the legislative body of the AKC, voting on rules and electing directors. The American Kennel Club maintains the Stud Book, the record of every dog ever registered with the AKC, and publishes a variety of materials on purebred dogs, including a monthly magazine, books and numerous educational pamphlets. For more information, contact the AKC at the address listed in Chapter 13, "Resources," and look for the names of their publications in Chapter 12, "Recommended Reading."

definite disadvantage alongside a cropped competitor. The optical advantage in elegance and length of neck afforded the cropped and erect ear is great.

THE NECK

Neck proudly carried, well muscled and dry. Well arched with nape of neck widening gradually toward body.

The Doberman's neck, while powerful in appearance, is never short and thick nor must it be set on bulky shoulders. The shoulders are long, flat and are what most dog fanciers refer to as "well laid back." That is, they slope back from the perpendicular at approximately a forty-five-degree angle. Bulging shoulder muscles belong to the Rottweiler and one usually finds overdeveloped muscle mass in the shoulder area accompanied by a short bully neck and bulging cheek muscles which totally contradict what the standard of the breed calls for.

The Doberman's body denotes muscularity and power.

THE BODY

Back short, firm, of sufficient width, and muscular at the loins extending in a straight line from withers to the slightly rounded croup.

The elegant, alert and powerful look created by the correctly made and proportioned Doberman head continues through to his ready-for-action body. There should

11

be no doubt in the observer's mind that the Doberman is ready and able to spring into action with split-second timing. While the breed's body type denotes muscularity and power, that power comes from a frame which one would associate with the body type of the human decathlon athlete rather than the weight lifter.

The Doberman is what is normally referred to as a short coupled dog. That is, viewed in profile the dog's length measured from the forward-most point of the chest to the rear-most point of the buttocks approximates the distance one would obtain by measuring the distance from the highest point of the shoulder blade (the withers) to the ground.

The Doberman's topline, the area from the withers to the set of the tail, must be level. One often finds the topline of the long-bodied Doberman described as a swayed back. Instead of being level the topline has a weak-appearing sag which detracts from the breed's fit, ready-for-action appearance. Nor should the topline be humped or roached. A topline of this kind denotes constriction rather than suppleness and flexibility. While the correct topline is flat, there is a very slight rounding off at the croup which is that area just preceding the set on of the tail.

As one would expect of an athletic frame of this nature, the chest and rib cage must be of sufficient breadth and depth to accommodate powerful lungs and a large heart but never so wide as to appear clumsy and over made. The chest should be deep enough to come to the dog's elbow and wide enough to hold those vital organs which will permit this canine athlete to work with not only great bursts of speed but also tirelessly for long periods of time.

TAIL

Docked at approximately the second joint, appears to be a continuation of the spine.

The tail is set so that it appears to be a continuation of the spine and is docked at approximately the second joint. When the dog is "on alert," the tail is normally carried at an upward angle, slightly above the horizontal.

LEGS AND FEET

Legs *Seen from front and side, perfectly straight and parallel to each other from elbow to pastern.*

Feet *Well arched, compact.*

All four of the Doberman's legs are strongly boned and muscular. The feet are tight, round and well arched, commonly referred to as "cat feet." The thick nails are always kept short.

A Doberman's movement is both effortless and powerful.

Forequarters *Sloping forward and downward in a 45-degree angle to the ground meets the upper arm at an angle of 90-degrees.*

The front legs drop in a straight line from the body, parallel to each other, turning neither in nor out, whether the dog is standing still or moving. Viewed from both front and side, the front legs are straight and strong.

Hindquarters *The angulation of the hindquarters balances that of the forequarters.*

The Doberman's hindquarters are muscular and powerful and, as one would expect, show no signs of excess or bulkiness. The Doberman's power to give a burst of speed, turn on a dime and leap to amazing heights and

13

distances all emanate from his hindquarters. The need for the hindquarters to be properly shaped remains without saying. The upper thigh meets the lower thigh at an angle which approximates the lay of the correctly positioned shoulder. This angulation gives the breed the ability to step out with strong and easy motion with great length of stride.

When standing still the line from the hock to foot pad should be absolutely parallel. With proper angulation of the thighs and perpendicular hocks, the Doberman's hindquarter is constructed in a manner to give him all the power, flexibility and efficiency required of this powerful canine athlete.

GAIT

Free balanced and vigorous, with good reach and good driving power in the hindquarters.

Checking the Doberman's gait is in effect a test of the breed's entire construction. It is absolutely impossible for a dog of any breed to move in a manner called for by his breed standard unless he is in effect constructed according to the demands of that standard.

When watching the Doberman move in profile, the reach of the forequarter is matched by that of the hindquarter. The movement is effortless, ground covering and powerful. The feet lift easily and clear the floor without difficulty, but the lift should not give the least indication of a prancing, hackney action. The topline holds firm and steady with no sag or sway. There is no bounce or roll from side to side.

Coming toward the observer, the legs move straight and true with no weaving about or paddling. As speed increases the Doberman "single tracks"; that is the legs begin to incline more and more under the body. Eventually the paws come to travel in an almost single line.

Moving away, the Doberman's rear legs follow the same planes as the front legs, thrown neither outward sor inward. The hocks should not incline inward or outward.

Coat, Color and Markings

Coat *Smooth-haired, short, hard, thick and close lying. Invisible gray undercoat on neck permissible.*

The Doberman's coat is a joy to the owner in that, when healthy, it is very low maintenance and requires little more than regular firm brushing and a quick wipe of the cloth. The hair is short, hard and grows tight to the body.

Dobermans come in many different color combinations. These puppies are blue, red and fawn.

Allowable colors The only allowable colors of the Doberman are black, red, blue and fawn. Fawn is also referred to as Isabella. Blue and fawn are simply dilutions of the colors black and red. A white patch on the chest is found on occasion but it must not exceed one-half square inch.

There are no other colors allowable for the purebred Doberman Pinscher. Any other color constitutes a disqualification under the standard of the breed. Dobermans of any other color should of course never be bred.

Markings All four of the allowed colors have clearly defined rust-colored markings. These markings appear over each eye, on the muzzle, throat and chest. The

15

markings are also found on all four legs and under the tail.

Nose color   Nose color corresponds to the color and genetic makeup of the dog. All black Dobermans have black noses and blues have dark-gray noses. Reds have dark-brown noses and the nose color on fawns is dark tan.

Faults

There is a clause which appears at the very end of the Doberman Pinscher standard which states that what has been described constitutes the ideal specimen of the breed. The statement goes on to say that any marked deviation from what has been described constitutes a fault and the penalty for a dog having that fault should be in one's evaluation of the degree of that fault.

For example, while the standard states the Doberman's back should be short and strong, not all specimens of the breed are so constructed. In evaluating the quality of the animal, one would only impose a minor penalty should the dog deviate slightly from what is described as ideal.

It should be clearly understood that a breed standard describes the perfect dog. However, there is no such thing as perfection in nature. All dogs have faults. Even the great show winners have faults, but theirs are minor in the overall picture. It should also be understood that most of these faults are purely cosmetic and do not affect the individual dog's health or soundness. Dogs with faults of this nature can make perfectly wonderful companions, but they should not be considered show-quality animals nor should they ever be bred.

Soundness of mind and body are without question the hallmarks of a well-bred Doberman Pinscher. No owner or breeder should ever settle for anything less.

The ideal Doberman serves as an intelligent, trainable and protective member of one's household. The well-bred Doberman commands and deserves respect.

chapter 2

The
Doberman
Pinscher's
Ancestry

Everyone reading this book has been attracted to the Doberman Pinscher for one reason or another. Either the look of the breed, the breed's reputation or personal experience has brought the reader to the point where he or she wants to know more about the Doberman Pinscher.

In order to truly understand any breed of dog, one should be familiar with the original purpose of that breed and the history of its development. This will tell you much about what went into making the breed as it appears today and will also tell you what to expect as far as character and temperament. The latter are extremely important considerations. The Doberman may *look* exactly like the ideal dog for you, but the breed's

17

Welcome to
the World of
the Doberman
Pinscher

temperament and needs and your temperament and needs may not be the perfect match.

These considerations apply to any dog. There are far too many dogs owned by individuals who are entirely incapable of providing the dog with the amount and type of training necessary to make the dog a good canine citizen.

The first point in favor of the person considering the purchase of a Doberman Pinscher is that the individual has decided upon a purebred dog. A dog of mixed parentage can provide as much love and devotion as a purebred dog. Unfortunately, in puppyhood, when most dogs join a household, the temperament, trainability and even physical appearance of a mixed breed are totally unpredictable.

The Doberman, like practically all purebred dogs, has been selectively bred for many, many generations to stabilize physical appearance, temperament and trainability. Of course there are variations within all breeds but by-and-large one can expect most well-bred Doberman Pinscher puppies to grow up looking like most other Doberman Pinschers and to behave with the same basic attitude toward the world. We can also expect the well-bred Doberman to exhibit the high degree of intelligence and protectiveness for which the breed is noted. This is a breed that is known to be quick to think and quick to act. While she bears a certain degree of aloofness to strangers the Doberman has a far greater need for love and affection from her owner than one might suspect.

Like all other breeds, the Doberman Pinscher has been specifically bred to excel at certain tasks. This one is in a performance of army-trained dogs at the Westminster Kennel Club show in 1945.

18

History of the Domestic Dog

To really understand a Doberman Pinscher one must understand why the breed was developed, for whom it was developed and the primary utilitarian functions that were prized and selected. With this knowledge in hand, the Doberman Pinscher owner is far better prepared to deal intelligently with the breed than someone with an "all dogs are dogs" attitude. That dogs all trace back to common ancestors goes without saying. However, the traits and characteristics selected through the ages make the character of breeds entirely different. These differences demand individual treatment.

To understand the Doberman Pinscher fully, it is necessary to look back far past the fairly recent foundation of the breed some one hundred years ago. Breeds as different as the Bulldog, the Borzoi, the Great Dane and the Chihuahua can all trace their ancestry back to the same source. When you stop to think about this for a bit you can't help but respect what humans have accomplished through the thousands of years they have inhabited this planet.

In the beginning there were wolves and cave dwellers. Now—well, just take a look around you. As difficult as it might be to conceive, Wang Foo the Pekingese and Czar the Doberman are both descendants of *Canis Lupus*—the wolf! Wang and Czar owe everything they are and do to the unjustly maligned ancestor of all dogs, the wolf.

WHERE DID DOGS COME FROM?

It can be argued that dogs were right there at man's side from the beginning of time. As soon as human beings began to document their own existence, the dog was among their drawings and inscriptions. Dogs were not just friends, they served a purpose: There were dogs to hunt birds, pull sleds, herd sheep, burrow after rats—even sit in laps! What your dog was originally bred to do influences the way it behaves. The American Kennel Club recognizes over 140 breeds, and there are hundreds more distinct breeds around the world. To make sense of the breeds, they are grouped according to their size or function. The AKC has seven groups:

1) Sporting, 2) Working,
3) Herding, 4) Hounds,
5) Terriers, 6) Toys,
7) Non-Sporting

Can you name a breed from each group? Here's some help: (1) Golden Retriever; (2) Doberman Pinscher; (3) Collie; (4) Beagle; (5) Scottish Terrier; (6) Maltese; and (7) Dalmatian. All modern domestic dogs (*Canis familiaris*) are related, however different they look, and are all descended from *Canis lupus*, the gray wolf.

People domesticated the ancestors of the wolf for specific reasons, to perform certain tasks. Some characteristics fit some tasks better than others. Humans bred dogs for traits that made their canine helpers perform tasks more effectively.

My studies have revealed that the disqualifications in many breed standards are placed there primarily for two reasons: First, to breed out the undesirable characteristics obtained from the crosses to other breeds and secondly, but probably more significantly, to eliminate from the breeding pool any animal which displayed physical or mental characteristics that prevented a dog from performing the task for which the breed was created.

Ch. Ferry v Rauhfelsen was the first Doberman to win Best in Show at the Westminster Kennel Club show in 1939.

Birth of the Doberman Pinscher

With this knowledge in hand, we can see that by the late 1880s dog fancier Herr Karl Friedrich Louis Doberman of Apolda in the state of Thuringia, Germany, would have had any number of well-developed and highly specialized breeds to choose from when he decided to breed a dog that would serve to help and protect him when making his rounds as a tax collector. It is said that Herr Dobermann was also keeper of the town's dog pound into which all strays, both purebred and otherwise, were incarcerated.

It appears he wanted a dog not so large as to be unmanageable but of sufficient stature to represent a threat to intruders and to perform her function as guard. She would have to have been an easy-care dog—smooth of coat. Above all the dog had to be alert, intelligent and possessed of great stamina and self-confidence.

At the time there existed a breed known as the German Pinscher that fulfilled many of the desired qualities sought by Herr Dobermann. Although non-descript in appearance, the breed was known for its aggressive and alert character. It was around the German Pinscher that Herr Dobermann was to create his breed.

Although not called by the name at the time, older specialists in the breed seem to agree that the "Dobermann" existed as a breed in some form prior to Herr Dobermann's dogs. However, they also agree it was truly Karl Dobermann that refined and developed the breed that was eventually to carry his name.

Herr Dobermann turned to both the Rottweiler and the old German Shepherd Dog (a much different breed from the German Shepherd Dog of today) for their tracking ability, stamina and intelligence. These characteristics were to become the Doberman Pinscher's legacy as well.

While the foregoing combination had produced a dog bearing the desired mental characteristics, Herr Dobermann was not satisfied with the look of the breed and breed historians seem to agree that Herr Dobermann and his disciples sought out the blood of the Manchester Terrier (then a much larger dog than it is today) and the Greyhound. The former was to improve coat texture, color and provide a smaller, darker eye. The Greyhound increased body height and skull length as well as greater speed and flexibility.

While it is suggested any number of other breeds was introduced into the Doberman gene pool, this is not entirely substantiated nor does it seem entirely plausible. Had the Doberman's gene pool been made up of as many breeds as have been proposed, she could not have become a stabilized type in such a remarkably short period of time as breed historian Philipp Gruenig notes. It appears that within thirty years of Herr Dobermann's early efforts, worthy specimens could be regularly accounted for every year.

Threatened in Germany

The very existence of the Doberman Pinscher in Germany was severely threatened with the advent of World War I. Because of the extremely adverse economic conditions of the war, a great many Dobermans were put down and the superior specimens were exported to countries not involved in the war. While this proved a boon to the breeding programs of the Dutch, Swiss and Czechoslovakians, it levied an almost irreparable toll on German bloodlines. Philipp Gruenig has said that nearly twenty of his best young specimens were either put to sleep or died of starvation when he was ordered to the front lines to fight for his country. Had the German army not needed Dobermans to assist in the war effort, the breed would undoubtedly have been entirely lost to German fanciers.

Dobermans are intelligent, highly trainable dogs. This one is clearing a long jump at an obedience trial.

Even with the end of World War I, the decline of the breed in Germany was not to cease entirely. The continuing severe economic conditions forced many of the breed's staunchest devotees to sell what remained of the best stock to the United States—at huge prices, but with devastating consequences nonetheless.

American money and interest in the breed, however, were to serve as a stimulus to German breeders, though recovery was slow. By the early 1920s popularity of the breed was soaring in the United States and scores of Americans were making annual Doberman pilgrimages to Germany. While many of the outstanding dogs were sold to America, the German breeders were clever enough to retain key dogs for their breeding programs. The adept breeders were able to continue to produce some outstanding dogs each year.

Ch. Tudor Wild as the Wind, "Indy," is evidence of what the breed has achieved today. She won Westminster Kennel Club's Best in Show in 1988, and is an obedience dog too.

The Doberman Pinscher in America

The *American Kennel Gazette,* the official publication of the American Kennel Club, included an organization called the Doberman Pinscher Club of America (DPCA) in its listing of clubs devoted to specific breeds as early as 1913. There was no significant interest in the breed, however, until the end of the World War I when American soldiers returned with dogs from Germany. The year 1921 marked the first official meeting of the Doberman Pinscher Club of America which exists today. The German standard of the breed was adopted by the DPCA a year later.

The 1920s and 1930s witnessed the arrival of practically every important German Doberman Pinscher winner to American shores. Clever breeders here were wise enough to follow German breeding principles and it was not long before the American-bred

Doberman Pinscher could stand alongside the best of Europe's product.

Still, the best of the German dogs continued to cross the ocean to America, culminating in the historic 1939 Best in Show win of Ferry v Rauhfelsen at Westminster Kennel Club under George Thomas. Ferry had arrived in America only three weeks prior to this win. Ferry's Westminster win was the first for Doberman Pinschers at this important event.

As American–German political relations became continually more strained, imports were dwindling rapidly. When European hostilities broke out in 1939 importing ceased entirely. The German source was totally cut off. American Doberman Pinscher breeders were forced to rely entirely upon their own ingenuity and breeding prowess. Even with the cessation of the war, American importing was never to regain the momentum it had through the first several decades of the 1900s. America had established such a nucleus of the world's most valuable bloodlines that, rather than putting Doberman breeding programs into decline, the early 1940s gave birth to some of the most important individuals dogs and kennels. In fact, American Doberman breeders were not only to prove they were able to duplicate and improve upon German quality, they were to all but eliminate some of the problems the great German imports had passed along to their descendants.

The early Dobermans imported into America from Germany were for the most part extremely aggressive. Ferry v Rauhfelsen was no exception. Ferry was an extremely aggressive, powerfully built male and was known to be an attack-trained guard dog. It is known that George Thomas, the Best in Show judge at Westminster Kennel Club, was so intimidated by Ferry that he placed the dog Best in Show without ever having laid a hand on him!

Ongoing incidents of Doberman attacks on humans earned the breed an intimidating reputation as untrustworthy and vicious. Undoubtedly out of patriotism, but no less detrimental to the Doberman, were

World War II's United States Marine Corps' claims that their Doberman "devildogs" were the biggest, fiercest and toughest dogs in the world. By the early 1960s the breed plummeted below the top twenty in registrations, a forty-year low point.

The Doberman Today

It is a tribute to the dedicated fanciers of this breed that they have, through intelligent selective breeding, been able to produce a dog that not only has all the intended physical characteristics of this marvelous breed but one with the steady, reliable temperament which has now become a hallmark of the breed. Gone is the "devildog" reputation. Today there are hundreds of thousands of Doberman Pinschers throughout America and the rest of the world whose primary function is companionship. They are trusted and loyal family members and most individuals who have owned a Doberman would never consider having another breed as a house dog.

This is not to say the Doberman has lost her birthright as guardian of the household. To the contrary. This is a characteristic of the breed to be held in the highest regard.

Introduced to family children early on, many Dobermans "adopt" them as their personal responsibility and, if anything, can become overly zealous in their duties. Raucous and rowdy behavior on the part of other children can alarm the protective Doberman, so it is wise to have the family Doberman in another area if roughhousing is anticipated.

The Doberman is, without a doubt, one of the most striking breeds.

The Doberman is a working dog and is indeed in her element when she is given work to do. The breed takes readily to protection and guard work. There are countless claims of the courage and resourcefulness of this breed in the area of guard work. Few intruders or intended thieves are likely to risk the wrath of a Doberman.

Many have proven themselves marvelous search and rescue dogs and still others have been trained as outstanding guide dogs for the blind. This is not to say that every Doberman born is suitable for work in these areas but those who do prove to be worthy candidates usually perform their duties without equal.

As quick to learn and athletic as the Doberman is, she is high on the list of dogs trained to teach and entertain. They have been trained as circus performers and a large number have become famous when used to teach young children correct safety habits.

Individuals who have been to dog shows and have been fascinated with the dogs performing in Obedience Trials will find no more trainable or successful candidate for high awards than the Doberman Pinscher. In fact, the whole training movement in America is credited to Dobermans and their owners as many of the early proponents of obedience work were Doberman owners.

And, as surprising as it may seem, the Doberman has also earned herself an admirable reputation in the hunting field! Some have been successfully trained as hunters and retrievers with an inherent ability to "point" game. Still others have been used for hunting such game as mountain lions and wild boar.

In the right hands, Dobermans have been trained as attack dogs but this is a highly specialized field and training in this area should never be attempted by any but the most experienced professionals.

Last but certainly not least, the Doberman Pinscher makes one of the most striking and glamorous of all the show dogs. Her slick lines, elegant carriage and free-flowing movement all contribute to a picture of undeniable beauty.

chapter 3

The **World**
According to the
Doberman
Pinscher

Owning a dog of any breed can be a great comfort and joy. Accompanying a pudgy little puppy through his many stages of development and along the road to maturity is an experience second only to that which parents derive from their own children.

Responsibility

What too few people realize is that, like having a child, owning a dog is a tremendous responsibility. The list of a puppy or even an adult dog's needs can be overwhelming to the person who has never experienced dog ownership. Human beings' desire to domesticate the dog and make him a homebound and loving companion has also

27

made the dog totally reliant upon human beings for his safety and well being.

Domestication has shifted the dog's reliance upon the canine pack to complete dependency upon human beings. Everything that a puppy was taught in the wild must now come from his human owner. A puppy allowed to do pretty much as he wishes when he wishes will become a rowdy nuisance. This can be overlooked in a Toy breed or small companion-type dog, but if large and powerful dogs such as the Doberman Pinscher are allowed to grow up without learning boundaries and rules of behavior they can be downright dangerous. It is crucial that a puppy learns his place as a member of the household from the day he moves in.

Is the Doberman the Breed for You?

Dog ownership takes a great commitment and is not something anyone should ever do on a whim. This is particularly the case in the ownership of a Doberman Pinscher.

All too often I read articles written by devoted and well-meaning fanciers of a breed in which they refer to their breed of choice as a "a dog for all reasons." I have never found this to be true in all my forty years of involvement with purebred dogs. And in the case of the Doberman Pinscher, I would find this description wholly inappropriate.

As we have learned, the Doberman Pinscher breed was created to be a bold and fearless watchdog and protector. Herr Dobermann, given credit as the breed's "creator," liked aggressive dogs. All the breeds Herr Dobermann brought together were those which would produce such a dog.

The overly aggressive temperament of the earliest members of the breed was mellowed through the addition of the more placid blood of the Manchester Terrier and the English Greyhound. Further, through judicious weeding out of dogs of untrustworthy temperament, the Doberman has become far more suited to a life as house dog and companion.

Given the proper guidance and training by his human "pack leader," the Doberman will become a wonderful companion and loyal protector.

This refinement in temperament has in no way diminished the breed's alertness, intelligence or courage. Properly directed and shaped, these traits can produce a dog which has no equal. *But* the kind of Doberman that has given the breed legendary status does not come about by accident.

The raw material the Doberman Pinscher is born with must be molded and shaped by his human pack leader. Done so and done so properly, the Doberman will repay his education by becoming an irreplaceable companion as well as staunch and loyal protector of home and hearth.

Loyal and Protective

The Doberman Pinscher is without a doubt, the most loyal of dogs. This is a breed whose greatest joy is to be alongside his owner. Spending a leisurely evening in front of the television set, riding in a car or taking a jog through the park make no difference to the Doberman, as long as these activities are in the company of his master.

Whatever belongs to the Doberman's owner must be protected at all costs, even at the expense of life or limb. A Doberman does not question the judiciousness of how he fulfills this responsibility, he only knows to comply.

A Doberman may become very protective of the children he lives with.

When "Cassie," the deceased Quilla's daughter, was about three years old we considered the possibility of adding a new dog to the household. We had become intrigued with the Bichon Frise, a breed that was relatively new to America. Cassie had been our only dog for so long, we had no idea how she would react to having a second dog in the house—especially a very small dog such as the Bichon.

After much deliberation we decided to try and see if it would work. We brought "Christopher" home as an eight-week-old puppy weighing about four or five pounds. Cassie was both intrigued and puzzled. Her expression read something like, "It smells like a dog, it sounds like a dog but—*that small!?*"

We kept Christopher safely confined in a small enclosure in the kitchen for the first week or so. In no time at all we found Cassie spending most of her day stretched out full length next to the puppy pen thoroughly enjoying little Christopher's charges and mock attacks through the fencing.

Our next step was to allow the two supervised playtime. To accommodate Christopher's diminutive size Cassie spent most of her time lying down on her back with the small white ball of fluff leaping over, around and on her body.

Cassie adopted Christopher and assumed full responsibility for his safety. Though *we* knew that Dobermans have no herding blood in their background, *Cassie* evidently did not, and took to gently nudging and pushing her small white charge away from any real or imagined harm.

Nor did we ever have to worry about some dog napper trying to make off with Christopher. Cassie made it perfectly clear that Christopher was definitely a "hands-off" situation in the case of strangers.

It was decided that Christopher would be given a chance to compete at dog shows. It was only after a professional handler was employed and our showdog departed on an extended show career that we realized how profoundly this would affect Cassie. She was crestfallen.

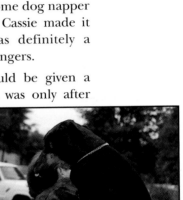

For days Cassie moped listlessly about the house, making it obvious we had deprived her of her best friend and playmate. It was only by sheer coincidence that we were saved from having to nip our now-winning dog's show career in the bud.

New neighbors moved in next door and as fate would have it, a

A Doberman's greatest joy is being with his master!

shaggy little brown and white dog they called Rags was part of the family. Cassie adopted her new "child" instantly and the two spent countless hours in play which included terrorizing the squirrels in the woods nearby.

In some mysterious way Rags broke a leg and was put in a cumbersome toe to elbow cast. Needless to say this severely restricted Rags's squirrel-chasing technique so she was forced to spend the better part of that spring lying on the deck behind her family's home.

Right beside her from morning when she was let out until late in the day when we called her home was Rags's good buddy Cassie. The two learned to play a very non-taxing ball game which consisted primarily of rolling a tennis ball back and forth between them. And when the ball went astray and rolled out of Rags's reach, Cassie became the retriever and would fetch the ball and bring it back into play.

*Doberman own-
ers must be sure
to teach their
dogs appropri-
ate territorial
boundaries, or
else they are
likely to set and
protect their
own.*

This went on until Autumn when Rags was liberated from her cast and she and her devoted buddy Cassie were again free to terrorize the inhabitants of the nearby woods.

As kind, loving and protective as the Doberman is, he cannot be expected to greet strangers with cordiality. After all, his very essence demands circumspection of those whose intentions are unknown. Until intentions are revealed, the stranger could well provide a threat to his master or his master's property.

It is amazing, however, how quickly the Doberman learns to sense his master's approval or lack thereof. Once a stranger is admitted and there is no sense of danger, the watchful, on-alert Doberman can quickly revert to an affection-seeking pest. The Doberman is a working dog and his work, at the risk of sounding trite, is to love, honor and obey.

The Need for Training

The Doberman puppy is all potential. How useful and obedient he becomes depends entirely upon his owner. The well-trained Doberman is one that is contented and well adjusted because he has been taught his place and knows what his boundaries are. Boundaries, both behavioral and territorial, are very important to the Doberman Pinscher. Taught early what he can and cannot do leaves little for the young Doberman to worry about. It is up to you to establish the boundaries by which your companion will live.

There was never a problem imposing behavioral boundaries on Quilla, our first Doberman. She always seemed to understand with the first lesson and seemed eager to please by obeying the rules or performing her repertoire of basic obedience exercises.

What we neglected to teach Quilla were our territorial boundaries. She taught these to herself and once this had near-disastrous results.

When Quilla first came to live with us as a puppy we lived high in the hills above Los Angeles. It is the range of hills that divide the San Fernando Valley from Los Angeles proper and are referred to by most Los Angelinos as the Hollywood Hills. In those days the hillside area in which we lived was very sparsely populated and, due to the layout of the roads, there was little traffic other than the few cars owned by local inhabitants. None of the homes had fences.

At about six months of age Quilla began a habit which she maintained for the rest of her life with us. At just about dusk each evening she would, as we called it, "sound the night alarm and go on duty." She did this by making a large circle around our home barking sporadically as she went along. The circle she made evidently established the perimeter within which she was on guard. While she was alert to strangers who entered the property during the course of the day, she was absolutely militant in her night patrol.

This was all well and good even to the point that her circle included a part of the public road that ran above our property. As I said, there was precious little traffic to be concerned about.

Late one night, however, we were disturbed by a commotion up on the hill. Shouts, a dog barking, scuffling. Next Quilla was in the drive barking her "do not pass" bark. But we also heard calls for our attention.

"Your dog just bit me," we heard a young man say in the darkness.

We were stunned.

After putting a very upset Quilla in the house we spoke to the young man who was with his girlfriend. He said that unprovoked, he had been attacked and bitten on the back of his leg by our dog while he and his girlfriend were taking a moonlight walk. He confessed the bite had barely punctured the skin but was upset nonetheless and of course we were very disturbed and highly apologetic.

CHARACTERISTICS OF THE DOBERMAN PINSCHER

Territorial

Energetic

Loyal

Needs firm guidance

Protective

We assured the young man that Quilla had been inoculated against rabies and that we had documentation to prove it which we could produce quickly. The couple were in a hurry to depart and living nearby, the young lady requested we bring by the rabies documentation the next day.

Bright and early the next morning we found the young lady's house and she answered the door telling us her boyfriend had already left for work. I showed her the current rabies certificate and turned to leave.

Just then the young lady said, "In your dog's defense, I think she was trying to protect me from my boyfriend."

"What do you mean?" I asked.

"Well, I was running down the hill. Tom was chasing me and when he caught up, he grabbed me by the shoulders and I let out a scream. It was all in fun but your dog appeared out of nowhere and threw herself at my boyfriend's back legs grabbing him by the pant legs. Her teeth just barely grazed the skin. More a bruise than a bite actually."

Quilla was defending what she believed to be her territory and evidently in her mind a state of emergency had arisen which called for protective action. This didn't make it any less frightening for the people concerned, but it became obvious to us that, lacking guidance from her owners, Quilla had established her own boundaries.

The Doberman can be a gentle playmate with small children, or an athletic companion to adults.

Living with a Doberman

The Doberman Pinscher is an exceptionally clean dog and most people find it an especially easy breed to housebreak. It is the rare Doberman that will willingly soil his surroundings. Referring to Chapter 8 and religiously following the instructions given there will result in a thoroughly housetrained Doberman in a surprisingly brief period of time.

Temperamentally the Doberman Pinscher is not an aggressive bully. Despite his size and power the Doberman can just as easily play gently with small children, puppies and kittens as he can rough house with another dog his own size or an active adult human.

35

Since the Doberman Pinscher is such an exceptional animal, the breed demands an exceptional owner to both appreciate his many qualities and be able to properly channel the breed's assets so they do not become problems.

The Doberman is quick to learn. It has been said that Dobermans are too smart for some of the people who own them. Owners can unwittingly reinforce bad behavior.

Never reward a Doberman who attempts to get something he wants by barking or misbehaving. Rest assured the clever Doberman will quickly realize and not soon forget negative behavior translates into positive results. He will then take you more time than you might imagine to undo that undesirable behavior.

Many of the things that attract us to the Doberman can become difficult situations unless those qualities are properly channeled. The breed is possessed of boundless energy. Therefore he must be given an opportunity for daily exercise. This is by no means a breed for couch potatoes. If not given time and opportunity for outdoor exercise, the Doberman will create ways to work off that surplus energy—some of which may be very costly to your home and furnishings.

One must not only be prepared to be loved by their Doberman they must also accept the fact that the dog demands physical contact to illustrate this devotion. The Doberman wants to be touched by those he loves and thrives on body contact.

Learning More About Your Doberman Pinscher

NATIONAL BREED CLUB

Doberman Pinscher Club of America, Inc.
Doug Jenson
2704 North Webb Road
Grand Island, NE 68803-1342

The Doberman Pinscher Club of America is ready to assist anyone interested in the Doberman Pinscher with questions they might have concerning the breed. Educational material, a breeders list and conformation and obedience clubs in your area are available on request for a nominal fee.

BOOKS

Adamson, Mrs. Bob, Brueggeman, John T., Denlinger, Milo G., Paramoure, Anne F., Sloan, C.W., Smith, Kenton E., and Umlauff, Gerda. *The Complete Doberman Pinscher.* New York: Howell Book House, Inc. 1972

Brearley, Joan Mc Donald, *The Book of the Doberman Pinscher.* Neptune City, New Jersey: T.F.H. Publications, Inc. Ltd., 1976.

Curnow, Fred and Faulks, Jean. *The Dobermann.* London, England: Popular Dogs Publishing Co., Ltd. 1990.

Doberman Pinscher Club of America. *The Doberman Pinscher Illustrated.*

Ladd, Mark. *Dobermans, An Owner's Companion.* New York: Howell Book House, Inc. 1989.

Migliorini, Mario. *The Doberman Book.* New York: Arco Publishing, Inc., 1985.

Walker, Joanna. *The New Doberman Pinscher.* New York: Howell Book House, Inc. 1979.

MAGAZINES

The Doberman Quarterly
Hoflin Publishing, Inc.
4401 Zephyr Street
Wheat Ridge, CO 80033-3299

VIDEOS

Doberman Pinschers
American Kennel Club

Living

with a

part two

Doberman Pinscher

chapter 4

Bringing Your
Doberman
Pinscher
Home

It is extremely important that the prospective owner not act impulsively when considering adding a Doberman Pinscher to the household. This relationship is one that may well last eight, ten or even twelve years. It should not be entered into hastily.

Where to Buy Your Doberman

It should be clear by now that a Doberman is not a breed whose bad habits can be ignored. There will be a leader and a follower in the relationship and, if you are not the leader, your Doberman can very quickly become an unruly and headstrong delinquent. The Doberman has a vast capacity to understand and learn, and it is up to you to provide the environment and treatment in which she may do so.

Therefore, your Doberman must come from a source that has concentrated on producing a mentally and physically healthy dog. This is best accomplished by going to a breeder who has a long-standing reputation for the quality of their dogs. This reputation is earned by breeders whose selective-breeding programs have been aimed at maintaining the virtues of the breed and eliminating genetic weaknesses.

The Doberman Pinscher Club of America is able to provide the prospective buyer with a list of private individuals who may have intelligently bred puppies for sale. Many local pet stores will also carry lists of responsible breeders they have dealt with over the years.

Good breeders are more than happy to have you see their dogs and to discuss the advantages and responsibilities involved in owning a Doberman Pinscher. Responsible breeders are as concerned about their dogs being placed in the right homes as you, the prospective buyer, are in having a sound and healthy dog.

Inspect the environment in which the dogs are raised. Sanitary living conditions are as important to raising good dogs as are good pedigrees. Never hesitate to ask questions and to see the breeder's mature dogs. The adult dogs will give you a good idea of what to expect in the puppy you obtain. Experienced breeders know which hereditary problems exist in Dobermans and are willing to discuss them with you (see Chapter 7 for more information on genetic conditions which may affect the Doberman). If the seller is willing to let you make a purchase with no questions asked, you should be highly suspicious.

Selecting a Doberman Puppy

Puppies should be happy, bouncy and outgoing. They are curious and alert, particularly with strangers. While not every puppy is wont to rush up to a stranger, beware the puppy that becomes terrified at the sight of someone she does not know. Quite frankly, I would be highly suspect of the puppy that cowers in a corner or panics at being picked up or handled. Do not make

PUPPY ESSENTIALS

Your new puppy will need:

food bowl

water bowl

collar

leash

I.D. tag

bed

crate

toys

grooming supplies

the mistake of selecting the shy Doberman out of some mistaken sense of kindness; a shy and frightened Doberman can easily become a dangerous and uncontrollable fear biter.

Instead, look for the confident puppy who pays attention to everything that is going on. Her eyes should be shiny and bright, her breath clean and sweet smelling.

Sour or offensive odors emanating from a puppy's mouth or ears is a danger signal.

We seriously advise against bringing a Doberman puppy home before eight weeks of age. At eight weeks puppies have usually been given their initial series of inoculations. Prior to immunization, puppies are very susceptible to infectious diseases which can be easily transmitted via the hands and clothing of people.

The friendly, alert puppy will grow into a loving and loyal companion with the proper guidance.

MALE OR FEMALE?

The choice between a male or female Doberman is primarily a matter of preference. We have owned both and while there are differences of course, they seem to balance out in the end. One important consideration is the size and strength difference. A fully mature male can easily weigh twenty pounds more than his equally mature sister and will have the additional muscle power to go with this size.

Our preference in a home companion dog in most all breeds has been for the female. They seem to mature mentally a bit earlier than their brothers and perhaps are a shade more gentle and affectionate as well. This seems particularly so in the Dobermans we have owned. Yet we know Doberman owners who say they prefer the male for some of these same reasons.

Unless the female is spayed, and we highly recommend that she is, she will have her bothersome semiannual heat cycles after she is ten or twelve months old. During these times, which usually last twenty-one days each, she must be confined to avoid soiling her surroundings and be closely guarded to make sure she does not become pregnant.

While both the male and the female must be house-trained, the male does present an additional problem. Males of all breeds, harking back to their wild ancestry, have the natural instinct to lift their legs and urinate on objects to mark and establish their own territory.

Both the female's heat cycle and the male's marking habits can be eliminated by having the pet Doberman altered, though this operation will not alter your pet's personality. (See Chapter 7 for more information on spaying and neutering.)

Your Puppy's Diet

The healthy puppy you have selected is in that condition because the breeder has been carefully feeding and caring for her. Every breeder has their own particular way of doing so. Our advice is to obtain a written record that details the amount and kind of food your puppy has been receiving and follow the recommendations to the letter. The diet sheet should also indicate the number of times a day your Doberman puppy is accustomed to being fed and the kind of vitamin supplementation, if any, she has been receiving. Following this procedure for at least the first month after the puppy comes home with you will reduce the chance of upset stomach and loose stools.

Usually a breeder's diet sheet projects the increases and changes in food that will be necessary as your puppy grows from week to week. If the sheet does not include this information, ask the breeder for suggestions regarding the change to adult food.

The Important First Month

There is much you can do at home to make the transition of the puppy as stress-free as possible. Remember, the new puppy has spent all of her short life in the company of her mother and littermates. The puppy will be lonely and confused. It is up to you to provide all those things that the puppy was able to get from her mother and siblings.

Anticipating the puppy's needs prior to the time she arrives and initially providing a place and an environment which will not be continually changing allows the youngster to acclimate much more quickly. Have everything ready before the puppy arrives so she will be able to begin the period of adjustment at once.

Before the day scheduled to bring your puppy home do two important things: First, arrange an appointment with your veterinarian so that you can stop there after you have picked up your puppy and before you bring her home; secondly, check with your breeder to find out the things your puppy will need to make the transition to her new home as stress-free as possible.

Veterinary Health Check   The breeder from whom you purchase your Doberman should supply you with a written agreement which states the sale of the puppy is contingent upon the puppy successfully passing a veterinary health check. Take the puppy directly to the breeder's recommended veterinarian or one of your own choice if the breeder's is not convenient. If it is not possible to arrange an appointment for the time you pick your puppy up, you should plan the visit to take place as soon as possible—certainly within the first twenty-four hours after the puppy has left the breeder's home or kennel.

Basic Needs   Prior to your puppy's arrival, take a trip to your local pet emporium to purchase the things that your puppy will require from the moment she first arrives in her new home.

Partitioned Living Area   We strongly recommend creating a partitioned-off living area for the puppy. Paneled fence partitions called exercise pens, about three or four feet high, are available at most pet shops and are well worth the cost for confining the puppy where you want her to be. The kitchen is an ideal place to set up this area as your puppy will miss her mother and littermates very much and will almost immediately transfer this dependence to you and your family. There is usually some member of the family in the kitchen throughout the day to keep the puppy company, and kitchen flooring is usually easy to clean in the event of an accident.

This fenced-off area provides an area of safety for the puppy as well. Not only does it keep the puppy out of mischief, but it also protects her from being bothered (or bothering) with older or larger dogs in the household. The adult dog with seniority may not be entirely pleased with the new addition at first. It is far safer to allow the two to get to know each other through the safety of a fence.

Puppies who have not been raised with small children may find these "miniature humans" very frightening. Most puppies love children but it may take a bit of time for the puppy unused to children to feel comfortable around them. The fencing keeps the child at a safe distance and gives the puppy an opportunity to accept them gradually.

Crate We always place the rigid fiberglass shipping crate inside the enclosure, the open door of which provides access to the dog's sleeping "den." These cages or kennels come in various sizes and while the one which will accommodate the fully grown Doberman may seem terribly oversized for the very young puppy, you will be amazed at how quickly your puppy's size will increase in just a matter of weeks. This crate will prove invaluable for both housebreaking and travel as well.

HOUSEHOLD DANGERS

Curious puppies and inquisitive dogs get into trouble not because they are bad, but simply because they want to investigate the world around them. It's our job to protect our dogs from harmful substances, like the following:

IN THE HOUSE

cleaners, especially pine oil

perfumes, colognes, aftershaves

medications, vitamins

office and craft supplies

electric cords

chicken or turkey bones

chocolate

some house and garden plants, like ivy, oleander and poinsettia

IN THE GARAGE

antifreeze

garden supplies, like snail and slug bait, pesticides, fertilizers, mouse and rat poisons

Some new dog owners will initially look upon the use of crates as cruel. More often than not, these same people come back later to thank us profusely for one of the best tips they were ever given, and their dogs have come to consider their crate as a private sanctuary.

Those of us who live in an earthquake-prone area find our dogs will make a hasty retreat to their crate at the first sign of a tremor. Often we have had to be very persistent to get some dogs to emerge from their crate even after the quake has long passed.

A dog's crate becomes a place of refuge if introduced and used in a proper manner.

Water Dish and Feeding Bowl   These are available in many different shapes, sizes and materials. We have found the stainless-steel non-tipping kind are easiest to keep clean and least susceptible to a puppy's chewing habits or to any attempts by the puppy to change her eating area into a swimming pool.

Food (as recommended on the diet sheet)   Supermarkets and pet shops carry countless lines of food for dogs of all breeds and all ages. Still, a breeder or veterinarian's recommendation will undoubtedly prove most beneficial in the long run.

Collar and Leash   Teaching your Doberman puppy to walk with you on a leash begins with the puppy's getting used to wearing a collar. Though the puppy may scratch at the collar for the first few minutes, she will very quickly forget that it is even there. We strongly recommend a rounded leather or nylon collar. Chain metal collars called "check" or "choke" collars are for training only and should *never* be left on your puppy. These chain collars are to be worn loosely and can easily catch on any number of objects causing injury or death.

We also recommend a four-foot-long leather training leash. The leather leash will last for the dog's entire lifetime (if you don't allow her to use it as a chew stick) and the length is one most trainers recommend.

Toys   Your puppy's toys can be almost anything you select just as long as they are safe. They should not have buttons or cords that can be torn off and swallowed. Avoid any hard toys, plastic or otherwise, that can be splintered. A good policy is to choose toys the puppy cannot fit into her mouth. This way you can be sure objects will not become lodged in the dog's throat or swallowed.

Never give your puppy old shoes, socks or any other items of personal clothing. A puppy cannot tell the difference between "old" and "new," and, once she becomes accustomed to chewing on articles that smell of her owner, she may find it perfectly all right to gnaw away on her mistress's dancing slippers or master's Armani belt.

Puppy Proofing

Your puppy's safety and your sanity depend upon your ability to properly "puppy proof" your home. In doing so you must remember that what a Doberman puppy cannot reach today, she may well be able to tomorrow. Doberman puppies grow like the proverbial weed and what you thought was out of harm's way may have been—a few inches ago!

Mouth-size objects, electrical outlets, hanging lamp cords and a host of other things you never looked upon as dangerous can be lethal to an inquisitive and mischievous puppy. If you look at your Doberman puppy as one part private investigator and one part vacuum cleaner, you will be much better equipped to protect your puppy and your belongings.

Puppies can get into places that defy the imagination. Many cleaning products, gardening supplies and medicines can be poisonous and must be kept in securely latched or tied cupboards out of a puppy's reach.

Many household and garden plants are poisonous as well. Your local agricultural department can provide you with lists of poisonous native plants that should be removed from your garden. Most plant nurseries will be able to provide you with information about poisonous house plants.

A product called Bitter Apple™ (it tastes just like it sounds!) is available at both hardware stores and some pharmacies. Actually a furniture cream, it is nonpoisonous and can be used to coat electrical wires and furniture legs. In most (not all) cases it will deter a puppy from not only damaging household items but herself as well. If Bitter Apple™ does not deter, there is plastic tubing available at hardware stores that can be placed around electrical cords and some furniture legs.

The fencing panels we recommended will help keep your puppy out of dangerous situations. A daily "puppy-proofing patrol" will help you and your pet avoid damage and danger.

Identification

One of the most important things that should be taken care of in the first few months is providing your Doberman with proper identification. Even though your dog lives in the house and exercises in a securely fenced yard, there is always the outside chance someone may leave a door or gate open and your canine friend may decide to explore the other side of the mountain.

Attach a small, metal **identification tag** with your address and telephone number to the leather collar which we recommend your dog wear at all times. Later, when your dog has been given her rabies inoculation, you should add this tag to the collar as well.

Collars and tags can be lost or removed so it is important to consider other, more permanent methods of identification. Tattooing and microchip implants are two possibilities.

A **tattoo** uses your dog's AKC registration number. No other AKC-registered dog of any breed has this same number so it positively identifies your dog. The only drawback to tattooing is that it cannot be done until the dog has reached maturity. If done as a puppy the skin stretches with growth and this may completely distort the tattoo.

Puppies can turn just about anything into a toy, so it's up to you to make sure they have safe ones.

Another possibility is to have your veterinarian inject a **microchip** under the dog's skin. These are about the size of a grain of rice and contain all of the particulars necessary to properly identify your dog. Most animal shelters and veterinary hospitals are now equipped with scanners that can read the information. Scanning is one of the first procedures followed by organizations so equipped when a dog arrives. The method is highly recommended by both humane societies and the AKC.

Training

Simple basic training should have begun the day you brought your puppy home. The Doberman puppy must learn the simple basics early on. The most important single command your dog will ever learn is the word *"No!"* It could not only help in avoiding any number of difficult situations, it could save your dog's life. It is as important for you to use this command only when you can enforce it, as it is for the dog to understand its meaning. Remember, a Doberman Pinscher learns very quickly. Once your dog realizes the "No!" command does not always apply, you are in trouble.

As the puppy becomes accustomed to her new home you can increase the number of important basics she learns. By the time your Doberman is six months old she should understand not to relieve herself in the home. She must learn to be left alone for increasing periods of time without barking or howling. Basics such as walking on a leash, heel, come, sit, stay and lie down can all have been mastered.

These are minimal lessons every Doberman Pinscher must learn to obey without a moment's hesitation and it is up to you to make sure your dog understands this. Chapter 8 deals with basic training and most trainers agree advanced training should not be attempted until a puppy is over six months old. However, what we recommend here are the simple

There is always a chance your dog may get out, so be sure she has proper identification.

basics that any puppy can learn without your having to be too intense about the training. Both you and your dog will be the happier for having these ground rules well established. Again, *never give your Doberman puppy a command you do not enforce.*

Exercise

The Doberman Pinscher is not for the sedentary owner. This is a plain and simple fact and is particularly true in your young Doberman's first year. Until your Doberman puppy is past a year of age she is not unlike a young child—possessed of boundless energy, stamina and youthful vigor.

If the young Doberman is not given ample opportunity to rid herself of this energy, if she is forced to harness this great capacity for action, you can rest assured the inventive Doberman will find other, sometimes very destructive ways of releasing it. Chewing, digging and finding ways to visit the other side of the mountain are alternate ways the bored and frustrated young Doberman has of unleashing her dynamo energy.

If your Doberman shares her life with another dog or with children, chances are she will get as much exercise as she needs. Dobermans, even the fully mature, have a sense of playfulness that seems best understood and shared by children and other canines. Unfortunately, not all Dobermans live in a household where they have these ideal playmates. A good many Dobermans are owned by adults who, like it or not, will have to accustom themselves to getting their canine friend out of the house at least twice a day for a brisk, one-mile walk. Your obligation to provide your dog with exercise exists through rain and sleet and dark of night. Exercise may not always be what you might prefer to do at the time but in the end it will contribute immensely toward keeping both you and your Doberman happy and healthy. It is simply part of the responsibility of owning a dog.

The alternative to exercising with your dog is to invest in a canine jogging machine. These treadmill-type exercisers can keep your Doberman in optimal condition, but it goes without saying it is an expensive way to avoid keeping yourself in shape.

As important as exercise is to the health and well being of your dog, it is important to use common sense in regulating it. Do not force a young puppy beyond her capacity. Young Dobermans use up their energy in short bursts with plenty of rest required between times. Their bones, muscles and ligaments are forming, and pushing puppies beyond their limits can cause serious permanent damage. Exercise programs for both humans and canines should be approached in moderation, with slow steady increases. This applies from puppyhood through to old age.

Tail Docking and Ear Cropping

Normally Doberman tails are docked and dew claws are removed at birth or within a few days afterward. This is done before the puppies' central nervous systems are fully developed and is accomplished with minimal pain and little or no bleeding. There are sound reasons for the removal of both.

Ear cropping is the owner's decision. Cropped or uncropped, the Doberman is an elegant and stately dog.

Dew claws are the additional claws that grow slightly above the feet on the insides of both the front and rear legs. These claws have no apparent function and are very easily ripped off in rough terrain causing injury and great pain to the dog. At just a few days of age the procedure is literally painless and takes just a moment.

The Doberman's tail is a barometer of her feelings. Those who have lived with the breed know it is basically a happy one whose greatest joy is being with its master. This joy is expressed through incessant and very vigorous tail wagging. While we Doberman owners appreciate the thought that inspires the action, these incessantly moving tails can clear off low tables in a few shakes and, even worse, strike solid objects with such force that the tail can be badly damaged or broken. There is no doubt in my mind that the Doberman is far better off without the tail.

On the other hand, ear cropping today is purely customary and cosmetic. There is no real need for the fierce look the founders of the breed thought ear cropping would produce. Many people think it gives the Doberman the alert and elegant look which has become a hallmark of the breed.

Ear cropping is a matter of choice best made by the individual owner but should never be done by anyone other than a licensed veterinarian experienced in this area. Each veterinarian will have a particular age they feel ear cropping is best done which usually falls between six and twelve weeks of age. At this age the ear muscles have not yet developed and they are more easily trained to stand erect after cropping.

All veterinarians who crop ears also have a regulated system of care and office visits which insure success and avoid the possibility of infection. It is wise to follow your veterinarian's system in all respects.

chapter 5

Feeding
Your
Doberman
Pinscher

The diet your puppy was on when you got him is the one he should begin with after you bring him home. The fewer changes that have to be made in the new puppy's diet, the less apt you are to run into digestive problems and diarrhea. Diarrhea is very serious in young puppies; they can dehydrate very rapidly causing severe problems and even death.

Regardless of age, if it is necessary to change a dog's diet, it must be done gradually, over a period of several meals and a few days. Begin by adding a tablespoon or two of the new food, gradually increasing the amount until the meal consists entirely of the new food.

Feeding Your Doberman Puppy

By eight weeks old, when you bring your puppy home, a Doberman puppy is fully weaned and is eating solid food. Prior to this time the breeder has gradually taken the litter from total dependence upon mother's milk to solid food consisting of kibble and meat.

Until about eight weeks of age Doberman puppies should be fed as frequently as five times a day. At eight weeks, the number of meals can drop down to four, and by twelve weeks of age three meals a day is sufficient.

The puppy will let you know when to eliminate the mid-day meal. If the puppy does not dive in and polish off the noon meal within ten minutes or so, pick up the food dish and dispose of the food. If this continues to occur you can dispense with the noontime meal entirely.

The amount of food you give your dog should be adjusted to how much he will readily eat at each meal. If the meal is consumed quickly, add a small amount with the next feeding and continue to do so as need increases. This method will insure that you give your Doberman enough food, but you must also pay close attention to the dog's appearance and condition as you do not want him to become overweight.

By the time your Doberman is a year old you can reduce feedings to one a day. Whether this is done in the morning or evening is really a matter of choice. The important things to remember are feeding the meal at the same time every day and making sure what you are feeding is nutritionally complete.

HOW MANY MEALS A DAY?

Individual dogs vary in how much they should eat to maintain a desired body weight—not too fat, but not too thin. Puppies need several meals a day, while older dogs may need only one. Determine how much food keeps your adult dog looking and feeling her best. Then decide how many meals you want to feed with that amount. Like us, most dogs love to eat, and offering two meals a day is more enjoyable for them. If you're worried about overfeeding, make sure you measure correctly and abstain from adding tidbits to the meals.

Whether you feed one or two meals, only leave your dog's food out for the amount of time it takes her to eat it—ten minutes, for example. Freefeeding (when food is available any time) and leisurely meals encourage picky eating. Don't worry if your dog doesn't finish all her dinner in the allotted time. She'll learn she should.

The single meal can be supplemented by a morning or nighttime snack of hard dog biscuits made especially for large dogs. These biscuits are not only highly anticipated treats but are genuinely helpful in maintaining healthy gums and teeth.

What to Feed Your Doberman

I have discussed foods and feeding methods with successful Doberman breeders in countries all over the world. Every breeder seems to have their own tried and true method. It appears the answer to the question, "What is the best way and the best food to feed a Doberman?" seems simply to be *the way that works best.* Common sense must dictate. Nutritious food is simply that, whether eaten by dogs or by humans.

An adult Doberman only needs one meal a day.

In order for a canine diet to qualify as "complete and balanced" in the United States, it must meet standards set by the AAFCO (American Association of Feed Control Officials). Most commercial foods manufactured for dogs meet these standards and prove this by listing the ingredients contained in the food on every package and can. By law, every container of dog food must list all the ingredients in descending order, by weight. The major ingredient is listed first, the next most prominent follows and so on down the line.

A constant supply of fresh water and a properly prepared balanced diet containing the essential nutrients in correct proportions are all a healthy Doberman Pinscher needs to be offered. If your Doberman turns his nose up at the food offered it is quite simply because the dog is either not hungry or not well. A dog will eat when he is hungry. If he is not well, a trip to your veterinarian is in order.

There are canned foods, dry foods, semimoist foods, scientifically fortified foods and "all-natural" foods. A visit to your local supermarket or pet store will reveal the vast array you may select from.

Truly nutritious dog foods are seldom manufactured to look like food that appeals to humans. Dogs do not care if food looks like a hot dog or wedge of cheese. They only care about how food smells and tastes. Since it is doubtful you will be eating your dog's food, do not waste your money on these "looks just like" products.

Most of the canned and moist foods which have the look of "rich red beef" or dry foods that are highly colored look that way because they contain great amounts of preservatives and dyes. Preservatives and dyes are no better for your dog than they are for you.

All dogs, whether Doberman Pinchers or Chihuahuas, are carnivorous (meat-eating) animals, and while vegetable content of your dog's diet should not be overlooked, a dog's physiology and anatomy are based upon carnivorous food acquisition. Protein and fat are absolutely essential to the well being of your

HOW TO READ THE DOG FOOD LABEL

With so many choices on the market, how can you be sure you are feeding the right food for your dog? The information is all there on the label—if you know what you're looking for.

Look for the nutritional claim right up top. Is the food "100% nutritionally complete"? If so, it's for nearly all life stages; "growth and maintenance," on the other hand, is for early development; puppy foods are marked as such, as are foods for senior dogs.

Ingredients are listed in descending order by weight. The first three or four ingredients will tell you the bulk of what the food contains. Look for the highest-quality ingredients, like meats and grains, to be among them.

The Guaranteed Analysis tells you what levels of protein, fat, fiber and moisture are in the food, in that order. While these numbers are meaningful, they won't tell you much about the quality of the food. Nutritional value is in the dry matter, not the moisture content.

In many ways, seeing is believing. If your dog has bright eyes, a shiny coat, a good appetite and a good energy level, chances are his diet's fine. Your dog's breeder and your veterinarian are good sources of advice if you're still confused.

Doberman. Dog food for the average Doberman should contain approximately fifteen percent fat and about twenty percent protein.

This having been said, it should be realized that in the wild carnivores eat the entire beast they capture and kill. The carnivore's kills consist almost entirely of herbivores (plant-eating) animals and invariably the carnivore begins his meal with the contents of the herbivore's stomach. This provides the carbohydrates, minerals and nutrients present in vegetables.

With exercise and the right diet, your Doberman will stay in top shape.

In nature carnivores are assured of a complete and balanced diet. Through centuries of domestication we have made our dogs entirely dependent upon humans for their well being. Therefore we are entirely responsible for duplicating the food balance available in nature. A dog's diet must include protein, carbohydrates, fats, roughage and small amounts of essential minerals and vitamins. There are so many excellent commercial dog foods containing these essentials available on the market today that many breeders feel it is a waste of time, effort and money to try and duplicate the nutritional content of these carefully planned products by cooking dog food from scratch.

What *Not* to Feed Your Doberman

Sugar, candy and sweetened pastries are filled with empty calories. Fed with any regularity at all, refined sugars can cause your Doberman to become obese and will definitely create tooth decay. There are no candy stores in the wild and a dog's teeth are not genetically disposed to handling sugars. Do not feed your Doberman sugar products and avoid products which contain sugar to any high degree. By this I mean if sugars of any kind appear any closer than halfway up the list of ingredients *do not feed it to your dog!* You will save yourself a lot of headaches and your dog a lot of toothaches.

Vitamin Supplementation

Finding commercially prepared diets that contain all the necessary nutrients will not present a problem. It is important to understand these foods do contain all the necessary nutrients your Doberman needs. It is not necessary to add vitamin supplements to these diets in ordinary circumstances. Many breeders' over-supplementation and forced growth contribute to the skeletal abnormalities found today in some pure-bred dogs.

Research indicates that while the Doberman Pinscher problems of Hip Dysplasia and Canine Vertebral Instability (also referred to as cervical spondylopathy or "wobbler" syndrome) are hereditary conditions, they can be exacerbated by overuse of mineral and vitamin supplements for puppies. These and other orthopedic problems which afflict the Doberman are dealt with in greater detail in Chapter 7.

> **TO SUPPLEMENT OR NOT TO SUPPLEMENT?**
>
> If you're feeding your dog a diet that's correct for her developmental stage and she's alert, healthy-looking and neither over- nor underweight, you don't need to add supplements. These include table scraps as well as vitamins and minerals. In fact, a growing puppy is in danger of developing musculoskeletal disorders by oversupplementation. If you have any concerns about the nutritional quality of the food you're feeding, discuss them with your veterinarian.

Most breeders we have spoken to feel that supplementation should *never* exceed the prescribed amount. Some of these same breeders advise that recommended dosages should always be halved. We have also spoken to some breeders who insist no supplementation should be given; that a balanced diet which includes plenty of milk products and a small amount of bone meal to provide calcium are all that are necessary and beneficial. Pregnant and lactating bitches may require supplementation of some kind but here again, it is not a case of "if a little is good, a lot would be better." Discuss this with your veterinarian.

Table Scraps

If the owner of a Doberman Pinscher normally eats healthy nutritious food, there is absolutely no reason why his or her dog cannot be given table scraps. What possibly could be harmful in good nutritious food? Several breeders I have spoken to advise a diet consisting of a well-balanced kibble base along with a small amount of meat (canned or fresh cooked) or table scraps of most kinds. The only table scraps which should not be given to your Doberman are those from food which humans should not have been eating in the first place. These forbidden foods include the previously discussed sugars, highly spiced foods and fried foods.

Table scraps should be given only as part of the dog's meal and never from the table. A Doberman who becomes accustomed to being given handouts from the table can very quickly become very persistent and annoying at meal time. You and your guests may find the pleading stare of your Doberman less than appealing when dinner is being served.

Special Diets

A good number of dog food manufacturers now produce special diets for overweight, underweight and older dogs. The calorie content of these foods is adjusted to suit each of these conditions. With the correct amount of the right foods and the proper amount of exercise, your Doberman should stay in top shape. Again, common sense must prevail. Too many calories will increase weight, too few will reduce weight.

Occasionally a young Doberman will be a poor eater. The concerned owner's first response is usually to tempt the dog with special treats and foods which the problem eater seems to prefer. This practice usually tends to compound the problem. Once the dog learns to play the waiting game, he will turn up his nose at anything other than his favorite food knowing full well what he *wants* to eat will be arriving soon.

Thin-coated dogs like the Doberman Pinscher can be susceptible to allergies and skin problems. Many of these disorders can be treated with diets formulated specifically for these problems. After diagnosing the problem your veterinarian can usually prescribe just which of these special diets would be most beneficial. Most veterinary hospitals also carry these prescription diets and they can be purchased by the case or in large quantities which makes them more cost effective.

chapter 6

Grooming
Your
Doberman
Pinscher

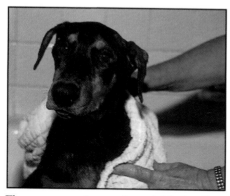

The owner of a Doberman Pinscher will never have to spend as much time grooming his or her dog as someone who owns a longhaired breed. But this does not mean the Doberman needs no grooming at all.

Frequent grooming allows you to inspect the coat for the presence of fleas or ticks. Fleas are a nuisance invariably leading to severe scratching externally and tapeworms internally. Ticks are able to transmit some serious diseases to human beings and must be dealt with quickly. Both of these parasites are dealt with in Chapter 7.

The Doberman sheds her coat just like the longhaired breeds do. The fallen hair is just less noticeable. Allow your Doberman to sleep on a white or light-colored sofa on a regular basis and you will be amazed at the amount of hair that leaves the Doberman's body in just a few day's time.

Brushing

Frequent brushing removes the old dead hair, cleans and massages the skin and allows the new hair to come in easily. The rubber curry comb is the ideal grooming aid for this project and your Doberman will quickly learn to look forward to this "massage." A chamois cloth, which can be purchased at most hardware stores, can be used to finish off your brushing job. This final touch will produce a high luster on your dog's coat.

If brushing is attended to regularly, bathing will seldom be necessary unless your Doberman finds her way into something with a disagreeable odor. Even then, there are many products, both dry and liquid, available at your local pet store that eliminate odors and leave the coat shiny and clean.

Brushing removes dead hair and provides a relaxing massage.

A damp washcloth will put the Doberman that has given herself a mud bath back in shape very quickly. However, should your Doberman's coat become wet in cold weather, be sure to towel down the dog thoroughly. The Doberman is a thin-coated breed and has no undercoat to protect her from a draft or winter chill.

Brushing should always be done in the same direction as the hair grows. You should begin at the dog's head brushing toward the tail and down the sides and legs. This procedure will loosen the dead hair and brush it off the dog.

Check the skin inside the thighs and armpits to see if it is dry or red. Artificial heat during winter months can dry out the skin and cause it to become chapped. Place a small amount of petroleum jelly or baby oil on the palms of your hands and rub your hands over the dry areas.

A grooming table that puts your dog at a comfortable working level will save your back and keep your dog still while you attend to her. These tables can be purchased from any pet supply dealer or can be built at home. Trying to groom your dog while she is standing on the ground is difficult at best in that the dog will be inclined to pull away from what she doesn't like and you will have to hang on with one hand while you work with the other. Sometimes you need to use both hands, particularly when clipping nails or cleaning teeth.

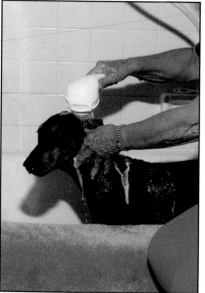

Usually brushing will do the job, but bathing may be necessary if your Doberman finds her way into something with a disagreeable odor.

Feet and Nails

Always inspect your dog's feet for cracked pads. Check between the toes for splinters and thorns. Pay particular attention to any swollen or tender areas. In many sections of the country there is a weed called a fishtail which has a barbed hooklike affair that carries its seed. This hook easily finds its way into a Doberman's foot or between her toes and very quickly works its way deep into the dog's flesh. This will quickly cause soreness and infection. It is best removed by your veterinarian before serious problems result.

To keep your Doberman's feet properly tight and arched, it is necessary to keep the nails trimmed regularly. Long nails can cause a Doberman's feet to become flat and spread. This is unattractive and the long nails can become deformed and cause a great deal of pain to the dog as well.

Do not allow the nails to become overgrown and then expect to easily cut them back. Each nail has a blood vessel running through the center called the "quick." The quick grows close to the end of the nail and contains very sensitive nerve endings. If the nail is allowed to grow too long it will be impossible to cut it back to a proper length without cutting into the quick. This causes severe pain to the dog and can also result in a great deal of bleeding that can be very difficult to stop.

If your Doberman is getting plenty of exercise on cement or rough pavement, the nails may keep sufficiently worn down. However, if the dog spends most of her time indoors or on grass when outdoors, the nails can grow long very quickly. They must then be trimmed with canine nail clippers, an electric nail grinder (also called a drummel), or coarse file made expressly for that purpose. All three of these items can be purchased at major pet emporiums.

Nail trimming is a necessary part of the grooming process.

We prefer the electric nail grinder above the others because it is so easy to control and completely avoids cutting into the quick. The Doberman's black nails make it practically impossible to see where the quick ends, so regardless of which nail trimming device is used, one must proceed with caution and remove only a small portion of the nail at a time.

Use of the electric grinder requires introducing your puppy to it at an early age. The instrument has a whining sound like a dentist's drill. The noise combined with the vibration of the sanding head on the nail itself can take some getting used to. Most dogs eventually accept it as one of life's trials. My dogs have never liked having their nails trimmed no matter what device I used so my eventual decision was to use the grinder as I was less apt to damage the quick.

GROOMING TOOLS

pin brush

slicker brush

flea comb

towel

mat rake

grooming glove

scissors

nail clippers

tooth-cleaning equipment

shampoo

conditioner

clippers

65

Should the quick be nipped in the trimming process, there are many blood-clotting products available at pet shops that will almost immediately stem the flow of blood. It is wise to have one of these products on hand in case there is a nail-trimming accident or the dog breaks a nail on her own.

*Most Dobermans
don't seem to
mind having
their teeth
brushed.*

Teeth

Giving your Doberman large hard dog biscuits and very large knuckle-type bones to chew on frequently will go a long way toward keeping the teeth clean and free of plaque and tartar. There are a number of inde-structible chew toys also available at pet shops which are very good in this respect as well.

Make a point of giving your Doberman the opportunity to chew on these recommended materials as plaque and tartar can build up quickly, causing odors and damage to the teeth. When this happens it may be nec-essary to consult your veterinarian for corrective den-tistry which is done under anesthesia.

Regular cleaning of your Doberman's teeth is also very helpful in maintaining sound teeth and gums. Use a mixture of baking soda and water to clean the teeth. It can be applied in the same way you would brush your own teeth and, surprisingly, few Dobermans ever seem to object to this procedure.

Eyes

Since a Doberman's eyes are somewhat deep set, mucus gathers in their corners, particularly first thing in the morning. This should always be removed quickly and carefully with a small piece of cotton. This mucus is normally a gray color. If it is any other color or if the eye appears red and swollen, you should consult your veterinarian at once.

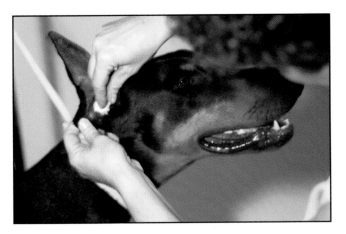

A Doberman's ears will need cleaning occasionally, but take care not to probe deeply into the ear canal.

Ears

Dobermans with cropped ears have relatively few ear problems because the ear is open to the air. Still it is wise to check and clean the inside of the ears regularly using a small piece of cotton moistened with rubbing alcohol and wrapped around your index finger.

There is no need to probe any further into the ear than your index finger will take you. Should you detect an odor or suspect a problem your veterinarian is best equipped to examine further.

Care of the eyes, teeth and ears is dealt with in greater detail in Chapter 7, "Keeping Your Doberman Pinscher Healthy."

Keeping Your
Doberman
Pinscher
Healthy

Regular grooming and aware-ness of any changes in your Doberman's eating habits or energy level will help you notice and diagnose medical problems before they get out of hand. The time you spend grooming your Doberman is the ideal time and place to do a close inspection.

Home Health Care

The first question to ask is, "Does the dog feel and look right?" A healthy Doberman is well muscled and very firm to the touch. If the flesh is flabby and loose or, on the other hand, you can feel your dog's spinal column and ribs easily, something is not right. The healthy Doberman's skin is tight-fitting and his coat is lustrous. Dull, dry hair is a sign of poor condition. Are there any unusual lumps, bumps or abrasions? These need looking into as well.

It is not a bad idea to keep a little record book noting any problems that arise and how they were dealt with by you or your vet. Should veterinary care again be necessary you may be able to assist diagnosis with the notes you have made in your dog's medical book.

This book is a good place to keep your dog's veterinary health and shot records as well. It will keep you aware of which inoculations are due and the dates they should be given.

Most veterinarians keep computer records of their patients and automatically notify owners of necessary follow-up treatment, but computers are computers and there are occasional glitches with the best of them. You should have your own record of when your dog needs heartworm and stool checks or when booster inoculations are required.

In this day of high medical costs, both human and animal, an ounce of prevention is most certainly worth a pound of cure. Pay attention to your Doberman and deal with problems as they arise—before they become serious.

Dobermans are, by and large, a healthy breed. Compared to a good number of other breeds they are what can be referred to as low maintenance. This does not mean one can be negligent. Dobermans are living, breathing creatures subject to various accidents and ailments as they progress from puppyhood into adulthood.

Knowing what to do when these problems arise is a very important part of responsible dog ownership. This chapter is written in the hope that it will assist you in determining the difference between situations that can be taken care of easily in the home and those that demand veterinary treatment.

Diet

As previously discussed, the healthy Doberman refuses all food when he is not hungry or not well. Should your dog go more than two or three days at most without eating, you should definitely consult your veterinarian. There are conditions that require special foods and it is important to your Doberman's health that you avail yourself of those your veterinarian might recommend.

The pet-food industry is both highly lucrative and highly competitive. Manufacturers do a great deal of research to determine the exact ratio of vitamins and minerals necessary to maintain your dog's health and well being. This applies to both dry and canned foods.

Like most things in life, you get what you pay for. High quality, nutritionally balanced food that is easily digested by a dog costs far more to produce than one that has only marginal nutritional value. A poor diet can lead to myriad problems. Do not economize in this area as it may cost you a great deal more to undo the consequences of poor nutrition. (See Chapter 5 for more information on nutrition.)

Vaccinations

Diseases that once were fatal to almost all infected dogs are now effectively dealt with through the use of vaccines. The danger of your Doberman being infected with distemper, hepatitis, hardpad, leptospirosis or the extremely virulent parvovirus is minimal if the dog is properly inoculated and the recommended series of booster shots is given.

Cases of rabies among well-cared-for dogs are practically unheard of in the United States. Still, dogs who

---

A FIRST-AID KIT

Keep a canine first-aid kit on hand for general care and emergencies. Check it periodically to make sure liquids haven't spilled or dried up, and replace medications and materials after they're used. Your kit should include:

Activated charcoal tablets

Adhesive tape
(1 and 2 inches wide)

Antibacterial ointment
(for skin and eyes)

Aspirin (buffered or enteric coated, *not* Ibuprofen)

Bandages: Gauze rolls (1 and 2 inches wide) and dressing pads

Cotton balls

Diarrhea medicine

Dosing syringe

Hydrogen peroxide (3%)

Petroleum jelly

Rectal thermometer

Rubber gloves

Rubbing alcohol

Scissors

Tourniquet

Towel

Tweezers

come in contact with wild animals can be at risk if not properly immunized. Rats, squirrels, rabbits and many other small rodents can be carriers of rabies and may be encountered by the city dog. It is very important to have your dog immunized.

Nursing puppies receive immunity to infectious diseases through their mother. The period of time between weaning and being inoculated to receive their own immunity is an extremely critical one. Puppies should never go to their new homes until the initial series of inoculations, called "puppy shots," have been given. It is critical that you follow your own veterinarian's schedule for all remaining inoculations religiously. Failure to do so could cost your Doberman's life. The age of your dog and timing of the inoculations vary. Therefore, it is critical that you discuss this matter with your own veterinarian on your dog's first visit.

All responsible breeders will have given your puppy at least one if not two shots against these infectious diseases before he leaves for his new home. Complete immunity can only be anticipated after the complete series of inoculations is given at the prescribed intervals.

> ## YOUR PUPPY'S VACCINES
>
> Vaccines are given to prevent your dog from getting an infectious disease like canine distemper or rabies. Vaccines are the ultimate preventive medicine: they're given before your dog ever gets the disease so as to protect him from the disease. That's why it is necessary for your dog to be vaccinated routinely. Puppy vaccines start at eight weeks of age for the five-in-one DHLPP vaccine and are given every three to four weeks until the puppy is sixteen months old. Your veterinarian will put your puppy on a proper schedule and will remind you when to bring in your dog for shots.

On rare occasions there are dogs that do not, for one reason or another, develop full immunity against infectious diseases. Therefore it is important to have the ability to detect signs of these illnesses in case your Doberman is one of the few who are not completely immune and actually do develop the diseases.

Canine Parvovirus   This is a particularly infectious gastrointestinal disease commonly referred to as "parvo" and can be contracted by direct contact or by exposure to areas in which infected dogs have been housed. While dogs of all ages can be and are infected by canine parvovirus, this disease is particularly fatal to puppies. Symptoms include acute diarrhea often bloody with yellow or gray-colored stools. Soaring temperatures as high as 106 degrees are not uncommon, particularly in puppies. Death can follow as quickly as one to three days after the first symptoms appear. Early treatment is critical. If there is any suspicion of this disease, contact your veterinarian at once!

Spend time with your Doberman and be attentive to things that may indicate illness.

Canine Virus Distemper   An extremely high fever can be the first sign of this very serious and often fatal disease. Mortality among puppies and adults who have not been immunized is extremely high. Other signs may be loss of appetite, diarrhea and blood in the stools, followed by dehydration. Respiratory infections of all kinds are apt to accompany these conditions. Symptoms can appear as quickly as a week after exposure.

Hardpad Considered to be a secondary infection, hardpad often accompanies distemper. A symptom is hardening of the pads of the dog's feet but the virus eventually attacks the central nervous system, causing convulsions and encephalitis.

Infectious Hepatitis   Infectious canine hepatitis is a liver infection of particularly extreme virulence. It is a different virus than that which effects people but affects some of the same organs. It eventually affects many other parts of the body with varying degrees of intensity so that the infected dog can run the entire range of reactions from watery eyes, listlessness and loss of appetite to violent trembling, labored breathing, vomiting and extreme thirst. Infection normally occurs through exposure to the urine of animals affected with the disease. Symptoms can appear within a week of exposure.

Leptospirosis Leptospirosis is a bacterial disease contracted by direct exposure to the urine of an animal affected with the disease. Both wild and domestic animals are effected by leptospirosis and can contract the disease by simply sniffing a tree or bush on which an affected animal has urinated.

Leptospirosis is not prevalent in all sections of the country so the problem should be discussed with your veterinarian, particularly if you intend to travel with your dog. "Lepto" can be contagious to humans as well as animals and can be fatal to both. Rapidly fluctuating temperatures, total loss of maneuverability, bleeding gums and bloody diarrhea are all signs. The mortality rate is extremely high.

Rabies Rabies infection normally occurs through a bite from an infected animal. All mammals are subject to infection. The rabies virus causes inflammation of the spinal cord and central nervous system. Rabies symptoms may not be as quick to appear or as detectable as in other diseases because they often resemble the symptoms of other less virulent diseases. Withdrawal and personality change are common symptoms as well as myriad symptoms accompanying the other infectious diseases already described.

Humans bitten by any animal suspected of being rabid should seek the advice of their personal physician at once. If your dog is bitten by a suspicious animal call your veterinarian without delay.

Kennel Cough Kennel Cough (infectious rhinotracheitis) while highly infectious is actually not a serious disease. It might be compared to a mild case of the flu in human beings. The symptoms of the disease are far worse than the disease itself actually is. The symptoms are particularly nerve-wracking because there is a persistent hacking cough that sounds as if the dog will surely bring up everything he has ever eaten!

The name of the disease is misleading in that it indicates a dog must be exposed to a kennel environment in order to be infected. In reality it can be easily passed from one dog to another with even casual contact.

In severe cases antibiotics are sometimes prescribed in order to avoid secondary infections such as pneumonia, but various protective procedures have been developed that can be administered by your veterinarian. In addition to inoculations, an intranasal vaccine is available that provides immunity.

These protective measures are advised for your Doberman, particularly if your dog visits a dog park or is taken to a boarding kennel. In fact, most boarding kennels now insist upon proof of protection against kennel cough before they will accept a dog for boarding.

Spaying and Neutering

All pet Doberman Pinschers should be spayed or neutered. As a responsible dog owner you would never allow your Doberman to run the streets nor would you ever consider turning him over to a dog pound or shelter. Yet, there is no guarantee that someone who purchases a puppy from you won't do just that. You would be amazed at the number of unwanted Doberman Pinschers found in animal shelters throughout the country.

ADVANTAGES OF SPAY/NEUTER

The greatest advantage of spaying (for females) or neutering (for males) your dog is that you are guaranteed your dog will not produce puppies. There are too many puppies already available for too few homes. There are other advantages as well.

ADVANTAGES OF SPAYING

No messy heats.

No "suitors" howling at your windows or waiting in your yard.

Decreased incidences of pyometra (disease of the uterus) and breast cancer.

ADVANTAGES OF NEUTERING

Lessens male aggressive and territorial behaviors, but doesn't affect the dog's personality. Behaviors are often owner-induced, so neutering is not the only answer, but it is a good start.

Prevents the need to roam in search of bitches in season.

Decreased incidences of urogenital diseases.

There is constant lobbying throughout America to restrict dog breeding because of the serious overpopulation that exists today creating an unending need to destroy unwanted animals. Thoughtful dog owners will leave breeding to experienced individuals who have facilities to keep all resulting offspring on their premises until suitable and responsible homes can be found.

If your female is not spayed, she will have her semi-annual heat cycles of about three weeks each, not insignificant hassles themselves. Neutering also significantly reduces the male dog's desire to lift his leg and urinate on household objects.

In addition to these benefits, spaying or neutering your pet *significantly* reduces the risk of cancer and other diseases. Your spayed female is less susceptible to breast cancer, pyometra and other diseases of the reproductive organs. A neutered male is not at risk of testicular cancer. For these reasons, it is clearly wiser for both pet and owner to leave breeding in the hands of the experienced few.

Use a scarf or old hose to make a temporary muzzle, as shown.

Muzzling

It is highly unlikely that a Doberman Pinscher will attempt to bite his owner, but any animal can snap in reaction to pain. You must not forget where you and I might use our hands in automatic response to pain, a dog will use his mouth and unintentionally injure the person trying to provide medical assistance. Therefore it is a good idea to muzzle your dog when administering treatment other than brushing or normal day-to-day grooming procedures.

We have always used a discarded nylon stocking as it is strong and will not cut or irritate the dog's muzzle.

Snugly wrap the center section of the stocking twice around the dog's muzzle. Do not wrap too tightly as to cause the dog to be uncomfortable but firmly enough to keep the dog from using his jaws to bite. Tie the two remaining ends under the jaw, draw them back behind the dog's ears and tie them there.

Using a Thermometer

Puppies, even grown dogs, are much like human infants in that they are unable to tell you when they are ill or if something is causing them pain. That said, there are telltale symptoms that are signals that all is not well. Loss of appetite, diarrhea, warm or runny noses, dull crusted eyes, lackluster coat and fever are some of the important ones.

Since fluctuations in temperature are a good indication of problems it is wise to have a metal rectal thermometer on hand. Metal rectal thermometers are best in that they are safer. Glass thermometers can break if inserted improperly or if the dog should react to the insertion by making a sudden, violent movement.

Sterilize the thermometer with alcohol between uses and always lubricate it with petroleum jelly before inserting it. We like to keep the dog in a standing position throughout the time we have the thermometer inserted. Properly inserted, the thermometer will slide smoothly into the dog's anus. It should go in about one inch. Never force the thermometer. This could cause serious injury to the delicate anal membranes. Allow the thermometer to remain about three minutes.

A dog's normal temperature (101.5 degrees) is somewhat higher than a human's (98.6 degrees). Both illness and excitement can cause a dog's temperature to fluctuate a degree or two either way but a rise in temperature beyond that is definitely a danger signal.

There is one rule that always applies: If you are in doubt as to how to handle any health problem, pick up the phone and consult your veterinarian. In most cases your veterinarian knows which questions to ask and

will be able to determine whether or not it is necessary
to see your dog.

Eyes, Ears and Teeth

If your Doberman's eyes, ears and teeth are checked
regularly as a part of the grooming process, there is
little else that needs to be done. If the eyes appear
red and inflamed, check for foreign bodies such as dirt
or weed seeds. Flush-
ing the eyes with cot-
ton and cool water or
a sterile saline solution
will usually eliminate
foreign matter.

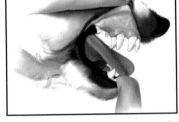

*Check your
dog's teeth
frequently
and brush
them regularly.*

Should the irritation
persist and the eyes
remain red, or if off-colored mucous is present, it
could possibly be conjunctivitis. Conjunctivitis is an eye
disease that is highly contagious and should be dealt
with by your veterinarian.

Anal Glands

The anal glands are located on each side of the anus.
Their secretion serves as a scent that identifies the
individual dog. These glands can become blocked
causing extreme irritation and even abscess in the
more advanced cases.

If you notice your Doberman pulling himself along
the ground in a sitting position you should check the
anal glands. Contrary to popular belief, this habit
is more apt to be the result of anal-gland problems
than of worms. While not a particularly pleasant part
of grooming your dog, regular attendance to the
glands will keep them clear.

With one hand place your thumb and forefinger on
either side of the anal passage. Hold an absorbent
cloth or large wad of cotton over the anus with your
other hand. Exert pressure to both sides of the anus
with your thumb and forefinger allowing the fluid to

eject into the anus covering you are holding. The glands will empty quickly.

Should you be unsure of how to perform this procedure or if your Doberman seems unusually sensitive in this area, it is best to seek your veterinarian's assistance.

External Parasites

Fleas No matter how careful and fastidious you might be in the care of your Doberman, fleas can still be a problem. Playing in the yard or even daily walks can bring fleas into your home and once there the little creatures multiply with amazing speed.

Those who live in Northern climates where there are heavy frosts and freezing temperatures have a winter respite from the problem as fleas cannot survive these conditions. Those who live in the warmer climates face the problem year-round.

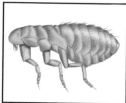

*The flea is a
die-hard pest.*

Unfortunately flea baths will not solve the problem. If you find even one flea on your dog, there are undoubtedly hundreds, perhaps thousands of them, lurking in the carpeting and furniture throughout your home. The minute your Doberman completes his bath, the fleas are ready and able to return to their host.

Aside from the discomfort flea bites cause your dog, the severe scratching they induce can cause "hot spots."

Hot spots are created by a dog's chewing and scratching so hard that the skin is broken. If not attended to promptly, these sores can form moist, painful abscesses and all hair surrounding the area falls off.

Fleas also act as carriers of the tapeworm eggs. When a dog swallows a flea, the tapeworm eggs grow in the dog's intestines. Unfortunately, if your dog has fleas he will almost invariably have tapeworms. The tapeworm is dealt with under the heading "Internal Parasites," below.

There is only one sure-fire method of keeping the flea problem in check. Make an appointment for your Doberman to be given a flea bath by your veterinarian or local grooming parlor. At the same time arrange to have a commercial pest control service come to your home while your dog is gone. The service will spray both the interior of your home and all of the surrounding property as well. Most of these companies guarantee the effectiveness of their work for several months and arrangements can be made for their return on a monthly or quarterly basis.

FIGHTING FLEAS

Remember, the fleas you see on your dog are only part of the problem—the smallest part! To rid your dog and home of fleas, you need to treat your dog *and* your home. Here's how:

• Identify where your pet(s) sleep. These are "hot spots."

• Clean your pets' bedding regularly by vacuuming and washing.

• Spray "hot spots" with a non-toxic, long-lasting flea larvicide.

• Treat outdoor "hot spots" with insecticide.

• Kill eggs on pets with a product containing insect growth regulators (IGRs).

• Kill fleas on pets per your veterinarian's recommendation.

While this measure does provide a solution there is a downside to the operation. Your home must be vacated and kept closed for at least a few hours following the spraying. Also there is the toxicity buildup of the chemicals used to be considered. Some services are now using a non-toxic method and it is to the obvious advantage of the dog owner to seek out these companies.

Flea collars are no less toxic than the chemicals used by most pest exterminators. While manufacturers attest to the safety of their flea collars, it is hard to believe constant exposure to these toxins can not be harmful.

The addition of garlic and brewer's yeast to your Doberman's diet can make your dog a less attractive host to the flea.

Great success in flea control is being achieved with the use of a relatively new, orally administered pill.

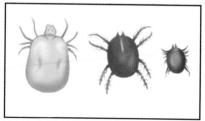

The medication, which can be obtained from your veterinarian, is given once a month and is proving highly effective in keeping fleas off your dog.

Lice   Well-cared-for Dobermans seldom encounter a problem with

Three types of ticks (l-r): the wood tick, brown dog tick and deer tick.

lice because the parasites are spread by direct contact. A dog must spend time with another animal that has lice or be groomed with a contaminated brush or comb in order to be at risk.

If no fleas are present and you do suspect lice, the dog must be bathed with an insecticidal shampoo every week until the problem is taken care of. Lice live and

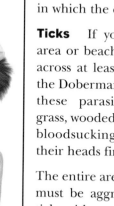

breed exclusively on the dog himself so it is not necessary to treat the area in which the dog lives.

Ticks   If you live near a wooded area or beach you are bound to run across at least the occasional tick as the Doberman can very easily pick up these parasites running through grass, wooded areas or sand. Ticks are bloodsucking parasites that bury their heads firmly into a dog's skin.

The entire area in which the dog lives must be aggressively treated against ticks with sprays and dips made specially for that purpose as they represent a serious health hazard to both humans and other animals. Ticks in some areas carry Lyme disease and Rocky Mountain spotted fever.

Use tweezers to remove ticks from your dog.

To remove a tick, first soak it with alcohol or another tick-removal solution. When the tick releases its grip you can remove it with a pair of tweezers. It is important to have the tick loosen its grip before you attempt to remove it. Otherwise the head may break away from the tick. If the tick's head is allowed to remain lodged in the dog's skin it could cause a severe infection.

Internal Parasites

Tapeworms and heartworms are best diagnosed and treated by your veterinarian. Great advances are continually made in dealing with both these parasites. What used to be complicated, messy and time-consuming treatments have been simplified over the years.

Tapeworms   Tapeworms are a part of the life cycle of the flea. If your Doberman has or had fleas he undoubtedly has tapeworm.

Common internal parasites (l-r): roundworm, whipworm, tapeworm and hookworm.

Small rice-like segments of the worm are often found around the dog's anus or in the stool. It is best, however, to have periodic stool examinations done by your veterinarian. There is an inoculation your vet can administer that quickly and completely eliminates the problem.

Heartworms   Heartworms are parasitic worms found in dogs' hearts. Dogs are the only mammals commonly affected. Heartworms are far more prevalent in warmer climates which have longer periods of time for mosquitoes to reproduce. The worm is transmitted by mosquitoes that carry the larvae of the worm. Blood tests can detect the presence of this worm and a veterinarian can prescribe both preventative and corrective measures, administered orally, for this parasite.

Whipworms and Hookworms   These two worms are shed in a dog's stool and can live for long periods in the soil. Both can attach themselves to the skin of humans as well as animals and eventually burrow their way to the lining of the intestines. They are then seldom passed or seen. These two worms are only detected by microscopic examination of the stool and each worm requires specific medication to ensure elimination.

Roundworms   Not an unusual condition, roundworms are seldom harmful to adult dogs. However, these parasites can be hazardous to the health of puppies if allowed to progress unchecked. Roundworms are transmitted from mother to puppies, therefore responsible breeders make sure their females are free of worms before they are ever bred. Roundworms can sometimes be visible in a dog's stool and are easily detected in a microscopic examination of a fresh stool sample by your veterinarian. The coat of a puppy affected by roundworms is usually dull, and the puppy himself is thin in appearance but has a potbelly.

A healthy Doberman's coat is free from mange and other skin problems.

Mange

There are two kinds of mange: demodectic and sarcoptic. Both are caused by mites and must be treated by your veterinarian.

Demodectic Mange   Demodectic mange (*Demonex canis*) is believed to be present on practically all dogs without creating any undue harm to the affected dog. Only about one percent of all dogs ever develop clinical symptoms.

There are two different forms of demodectic mange: local and general. Dogs affected locally may lose the hair around their eyes and in small patches on the chest and forelegs. This form can be easily treated by a veterinarian and must not be neglected because on rare occasions the local form can develop into the more severe generalized form

Sarcoptic Mange Sarcoptic mange (*Sarcoptes sca-biei var canis*) is also known as scabies and can be present over the entire dog. Symptoms include loss of hair on legs and ears, often in patches over the entire body. Your veterinarian must do a skin scraping to identify the type and prescribe treatment. Weekly bathing with medications especially formulated for this parasite can usually eliminate the problem. This type of mange is passed on by direct contact and is highly contagious.

Administering Medications

Ointments, Ear and Eye Medications Tubes with nozzle applicators help aim the medication exactly where you want it to go and can make sure it finds its

Squeeze eye oint-ment into the lower lid.

way into the eye or down the ear canal. This type of tube also helps get ointments into punctures or cuts. Again, it is wise to muzzle your Doberman if applying an ointment which might sting or burn. The inside of a Doberman's ear is particularly sensitive and the application of medication there can sometimes be startling to the dog.

Pills While there are a number of ways to get a pill down your dog's throat, I have found the fine art of deception works best. I disguise the pill in a bit of the dog's favorite food or snack. While I certainly do not recommend sugar as a mainstay in

To give a pill, open the mouth wide, then drop it in the back of the throat.

your Doberman's diet, rolling the pill up in a bit of soft candy can get the pill over the tongue and down the throat in a second and certainly beats trying to wrestle your friend into submission.

Cheese or tuna will work equally well if they are on your Doberman's top-ten treats list. I usually give my dogs a pill-free sample of the food first to whet their appetite; this insures the second treat containing the pill will be wolfed down without hesitation.

Putting medication in a dog's food and assuming it has been eaten is not a good idea. More than once I have seen dogs seek out the tiniest of pills from the food dish and discard them on the other side of the room.

Liquids   Trying to put a spoonful of medicine into your dog's mouth can be a bigger chore than you might imagine, especially if the medicine has a taste your dog dislikes. A turkey baster (or a syringe if there is only a small amount of liquid) can solve the problem easily.

It is best to shoot the medication into the side of the dog's mouth or under the tongue. Avoid shooting any liquids directly into the throat area as the dog could easily choke.

Emergency Situations

POISONS

Some of the many household substances harmful to your dog.

Always keep the telephone numbers of your local poison-control center and the local twenty-four-hour emergency veterinary hospital current and easily available. If you do know or suspect which poison your dog has ingested give this information to the poison-control center, they may be able to prescribe an immediate antidote. Do pass on to your veterinarian any information the poison-control center gives you.

If you are not sure if your dog has been poisoned, or do not know which poison he may have ingested, be prepared to describe the symptoms to the poison-control center or your veterinarian.

Common symptoms of poisoning are: paralysis, convulsions, tremors, diarrhea, vomiting and stomach cramps accompanied by howling, heavy breathing and whimpering.

STINGS AND BITES# STINGS AND BITES

Dobermans are forever curious and will give crawling and flying insects more attention than they deserve. This often results in potentially harmful stings and bites around the feet or, even worse, around the mouth and nose.

Visible stingers can be removed with a pair of tweezers. Once removed, apply a saline solution or mild antiseptic. If the swelling is large, particularly inside the mouth, or if the dog appears to be in shock, consult your veterinarian at once.

SKUNKS AND PORCUPINES

If your suburban or country Doberman fashions himself a "great black (or red) hunter," he can easily come in contact with skunks and porcupines. Both encounters can have disagreeable, sometimes dangerous consequences.

Skunks While your dog may not particularly enjoy his encounter with a skunk, you will enjoy it even less as the odor is not exactly Chanel No. 5. There are many commercial products sold by pet emporiums which will eliminate the odor quickly and thoroughly. If you are unable to obtain one of these products when you need it, tomato juice is a handy and effective remedy. Spray the dog thoroughly with the juice, allowing it to remain on the coat for approximately twenty minutes, then rinse off and, if possible, allow the dog to dry in the sun.

Odor is not the only problem resulting from an encounter with a skunk. Reports of rabid skunks are alarmingly high and skunks are not the least timid about defending

---

WHEN TO CALL THE VET

In any emergency situation, you should call your veterinarian immediately. You can make the difference in your dog's life by staying as calm as possible when you call and by giving the doctor or the assistant as much information as possible before you leave for the clinic. That way, the vet will be able to take immediate, specific action to remedy your dog's situation.

Emergencies include acute abdominal pain, suspected poisoning, snakebite, burns, frostbite, shock, dehydration, abnormal vomiting or bleeding, and deep wounds. You are the best judge of your dog's health, as you live with and observe him every day. Don't hesitate to call your veterinarian if you suspect trouble.

themselves. If skunks are present in your area or if you plan on taking your dog to an area where skunks may be found, be sure to have your Doberman's rabies shots up-to-date.

Porcupines   If your dog has been the recipient of the porcupine's defense, do not attempt to remove the quills by yourself. Get your dog to a veterinarian at once.

In the unfortunate event that you are unable to get your dog to a veterinarian, do your best to muzzle him before you attempt to do anything at all. Cut the quills back to an inch or two and remove them with pliers, pulling them out with a straight, forward motion.

Run your hands regularly over your dog to feel for any injuries.

Shock

As careful as we might be, puppies and young dogs always seem able to find an electric cord to chew on which can result in shock. If the dog has collapsed, hold ammonia under his nose or begin artificial respiration at once.

To give a Doberman artificial respiration, place the dog on his side with his head low and press on the abdomen and rib cage, releasing pressure at intervals of about one or two seconds. Keep the shocked dog as warm as possible and call your veterinarian at once.

Foreign Objects

Dogs, especially young ones, seem to have a need to scoop up small objects they find on the floor or in the garden and get them into their mouths. Often these objects will get lodged or trapped across their teeth, usually halfway back or even where the two jaws hinge. If you see your Doberman pawing at his mouth or rubbings his jaws along the ground, check to see if there is something lodged in the dog's mouth.

Should this be the case, grasp the object firmly between your fingers and push firmly toward the back of the mouth where the teeth are wider apart. This normally dislodges the object but be sure to have a firm grip on the object so the dog does not swallow it. If the object does not come loose immediately get your Doberman to the veterinarian at once.

If the object may have already been swallowed, investigate to see if it is still present in the dog's throat. If so, grasp the object firmly and pull it out. If the dog seems to be having trouble breathing, the object could be lodged in the windpipe. Sharp blows to the rib cage can help make the dog expel air from the lungs and expel the object as well.

Whenever any small object is missing in the home and you suspect your Doberman has swallowed it, consult your veterinarian. X rays can normally reveal the "treasure" and save your dog's life.

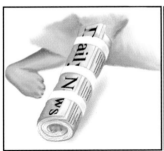 

Make a temporary splint by wrapping the leg in firm casing, then bandaging it.

ACCIDENTS

In the event of a road accident, it is extremely important that you remain calm. If not handled correctly and immediately, injuries sustained by your Doberman when hit by an automobile or motorcycle can be fatal. Panic on your part can upset the animal even further and cause him to thrash about and injure himself even more.

Should your dog be unable to move, try to obtain assistance in moving him out of the road. Make every effort to support the dog's body as much as possible. If a blanket or coat is available, slip this under the dog and move the injured animal in this manner.

Do not attempt to determine how serious the injuries may be. Often there is internal bleeding and damage which you are unable to detect. Get your dog to the veterinarian's office at once. Again, if there is someone available to drive you and your dog to the veterinary hospital, all the better in that you will then be able to devote your attention to keeping the dog calm and as immobile as possible.

BLEEDING WOUNDS

If your dog is bleeding you must attend to the wounds at once. If the flow of blood is not stemmed your

An Elizabethan collar keeps your dog from licking a fresh wound.

dog could bleed to death. Apply pressure directly to the bleeding point with a cotton pad or compress soaked in cold water. If bleeding continues you must seek your veterinarian's advise.

Should your Doberman be bitten by another dog get him to the veterinarian without delay. Even the most minor bite wounds can be infected and should get antibiotic treatment without delay.

Vomiting and Diarrhea

It seems the most common canine ailments are vomiting and diarrhea. This does not necessarily mean your dog is seriously ill, but should either symptom persist, call your veterinarian. Dogs purge their digestive tracts by vomiting. Puppies often do this when they have eaten too much or too fast. Even nervousness or fright can induce vomiting. None of this is cause for alarm unless it occurs repeatedly.

Occasional diarrhea is best treated by switching your dog's regular diet to thoroughly cooked rice with a very small amount of boiled chicken. Keep your dog on this diet until the condition improves and then gradually return your dog to his normal diet.

If either of these condition persist, however, or if you notice other symptoms, contact your veterinarian immediately.

Genetic Predispositions

Like all breeds of domesticated dogs, Doberman Pinschers have their share of hereditary problems. Those of us who control the breeding of our domesticated dogs are intent upon saving all the puppies in a litter, even those which left to nature would not make it beyond a few days. Our humanitarian proclivities have a down side as well. In saving life we also perpetuate health problems.

The diseases or disorders described here may not be present in the Doberman you buy or in his immediate ancestors. These are problems that do exist in the breed, however, and should be discussed with the breeder from whom you purchase your dog. A reputable Doberman breeder is well aware of these problems and should be more than willing to discuss them with you.

Cervical Vertebral Instability   Cervical Vertebral Instability, commonly referred to as CVI or "Wobbler Syndrome," is a misalignment of the cervical vertebrae which causes loss of control of the dog's limbs, particularly the hindquarters. Early symptoms include lack of coordination and stumbling. Eventually the affected dog drags his hindquarters and in advanced cases even the forelegs are affected.

It is of course very important that the puppy you purchase be from breeding stock which has been radiologically tested to detect this condition as its cause appears to be the result of heredity, environment and nutrition. Many Doberman breeders feel the condition can be exacerbated by over-supplementing a growing dog's diet as was discussed in Chapter 5, "Feeding Your Doberman Pinscher."

Hip Dysplasia   This is a developmental disease of the hip joint. The result is instability of the joint due to abnormal contours of one or both of the hip joints. Affected dogs might show tenderness in the hip, walk with a limp or swaying gait or experience difficulty when getting up after sleeping. The syndrome first appears during growing stages and usually becomes progressively worse as the dog grows older.

Again, controversy surrounds this disease regarding its genetic basis. It is now believed that while propensity

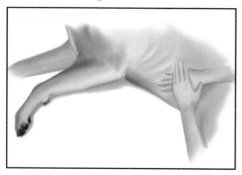

Applying abdominal thrusts can save a choking dog.

for the condition can be inherited it is yet another condition which can be promoted by improper feeding and over-supplementation in puppies and young dogs.

Surgery to replace affected hips has been developed. All breeding stock and any Doberman who exhibits suspicious symptoms should be x-rayed and the problem discussed with both the breeder from whom you purchase your dog and your veterinarian.

Cardiomyopathy Cardiomyopathy results in sudden death by complete heart failure or progressive deterioration of the heart muscle which is also fatal. It is a serious problem in Doberman Pinschers with an extremely high percentage of the breed, particularly the male population, dying from the disease each year. It is an accepted fact that the disease occurs regularly in certain lines of this breed and extensive research is being conducted to determine the mode of inheritance. Conscientious breeders test extensively to eliminate this problem from the breeding stock. It behooves the prospective Doberman Pinscher owner to be extremely selective about where their dog is purchased.

Von Willebrand's Disease Von Willebrand's Disease, referred to as "VWD," is an abnormal condition of the blood-clotting system which is similar to, but in most cases not as severe, as hemophilia in human beings. Dobermans are one of the many breeds which can be afflicted with this disease. It is seldom fatal in itself but can present a serious problem if surgery of any kind becomes necessary because uncontrolled bleeding can occur.

Stress can bring on this condition which is evidenced by mild bleeding from the nose and gums and occasionally bloody stools or urine. Research has revealed there is some evidence that clinical severity of VWD decreases with age.

Bloat   While bloat (gastric torsion) is not actually known to be an inherited problem, it does occur in deep-chested breeds such as the Doberman Pinscher with enough regularity to warrant considering. Little is known about the actual cause of bloat. Many theories have been offered but none actually proven. This often fatal condition seems to occur frequently at night after the dog has had a large meal, ingested a great deal of water and then exercises strenuously.

Symptoms can range from a severe attack of gas to death. It can occur so suddenly that only immediate attention by a veterinarian experienced with the condition will save your dog's life.

Simply described, bloat causes the stomach to rotate so that both ends are closed off. The food contained in the stomach ferments but gasses can not escape thereby causing the stomach to swell, greatly pressuring the entire diaphragm and consequently leading to extreme cardiac and respiratory complications. The affected dog is in extreme pain and death can follow very quickly unless the gas is released through surgery.

Blue Dobe Syndrome   This is a chronic skin condition of Blue Doberman Pinschers alone. The blue color as described in Chapter 1, "What Is a Doberman Pinscher?," is simply a dilution of the color black. Unfortunately the color can be genetically linked to some unfortunate conditions. Puppies may exhibit this condition at birth giving a moth-eaten appearance.

Bald patches can become evident by twelve weeks of age and small abscesses may also be present.

Symptoms of Blue Dobe Syndrome can be treated with regular medicated shampoos and topical medications with some success. The condition itself, however, has proven incurable. In addition to the disagreeable appearance of the afflicted dog, it appears there is an inability on the part of the dog to metabolize zinc. This inability makes the dog highly susceptible to staph infection and prevents the development of a normal immunization system.

The aging Doberman will need less food and more rest, but the same amount of affection and attention.

Bare Patches Doberman Pinschers and other short and single-coated breeds often lose hair in patches on the body and at the base of the tail. This hereditary condition is called Hormonal Alopecia and is caused by an imbalance in the animal's hormone secretions. There is no soreness, infection or skin eruptions, only hair loss. Detection of vitamin and/or mineral deficiencies can often assist in the treatment of this problem.

The Aging Doberman

Old age (neither yours nor your Doberman's) should provide an exemption from exercise. Exercise will need to be approached with moderation. Approached in this manner, it will undoubtedly add years to the relationship that has been established than if the two of you were to sit in front of the television set eating popcorn.

Diet, of course, should be altered for the aging Doberman. Less food and less protein will be required even though the old timer may have ideas to the contrary. Here the choice is yours—you can gratify your aging dog's desire for more food than he needs and lessen the time he will be with you, or resist the temptation to do so and keep the old timer on a diet that will stave off obesity.

The need for more daytime rest increases with age and you will undoubtedly find your geriatric Doberman seeking out a soft, warm place to nap more and more frequently. Aging also affects the Doberman's ability to see and hear. Do make concessions if you find your previously obedient companion failing to respond quickly or not at all.

The old timer's patience may wear through more quickly than it did when he was a youngster. Children and puppies can aggravate the old dog and steps should be taken to make sure this doesn't happen.

Veterinary science has developed many new ways to help your dog stay reasonably fit and healthy even on into advanced years. Regular veterinary visits can help prevent the rapid progress of ailments that lead to the deterioration of the geriatric Doberman.

THE LAST GOOD-BYE

Eventually there will come a time, however, when your long-time companion is no longer able to enjoy life and you must make a painful decision. Fortunately, when science can no longer prevent our canine friend's suffering or incontinence, we are able to bring his life to a close mercifully.

Your veterinarian is best equipped to tell you when this time has come and it is wise to follow his or her advice. Veterinary medicine has devised ways to bring your pet's life to a close with tenderness and skill.

Done professionally there is no stress to your dog, especially if you are there to comfort the dog while the veterinarian administers the injection. This is never an easy decision to make but it is without a doubt the kindest action you can take after your canine friend has given you so many years of companionship and pleasure.

Your Happy, Healthy Pet

Your Dog's Name _____

Name on Your Dog's Pedigree (if your dog has one) _____

_____

Where Your Dog Came From _____

_____

Your Dog's Birthday _____

Your Dog's Veterinarian

    Name _____

    Address _____

    Phone Number_____

    Emergency Number_____

Your Dog's Health

    Vaccines

    type _____ date given _____

    type _____ date given _____

    type _____ date given _____

    type _____ date given _____

    Heartworm

    date tested _____ type used_____ start date _____

Your Dog's License Number_____

Groomer's Name and Number _____

Dogsitter/Walker's Name and Number_____

Awards Your Dog Has Won

    Award _____ date earned _____

    Award _____ date earned _____

part three

Enjoying

your

Dog

chapter 8

Basic
Training

by Ian Dunbar, Ph.D., MRCVS

Training is the jewel in the crown—the most important aspect of doggy husbandry. There is no more important variable influencing dog behavior and temperament than the dog's education: A well-trained, well-behaved and good-natured puppydog is always a joy to live with, but an untrained and uncivilized dog can be a perpetual nightmare. Moreover, deny the dog an education and it will not have the opportunity to fulfill its own canine potential; neither will it have the ability to communicate effectively with its human companions.

Luckily, modern psychological training methods are easy, efficient and effective and, above all, considerably dog-friendly and user-friendly. Doggy education is as simple as it is enjoyable. But before you can have a good time play-training with your new dog, you have to learn what to do and how to do it. There is no bigger variable influencing the success of dog training than the *owner's* experience and expertise. *Before you embark on the dog's education, you must first educate yourself.*

Basic Training for Owners

Ideally, basic owner training should begin well *before* you select your dog. Find out all you can about your chosen breed first, then master rudimentary training and handling skills. If you already have your puppy/dog, owner training is a dire emergency—the clock is running! Especially for puppies, the first few weeks at home are the most important and influential days in the dog's life. Indeed, the cause of most adolescent and adult problems may be traced back to the initial days the pup explores his new home. This is the time to establish the *status quo*—to teach the puppy/dog how you would like him to behave and so prevent otherwise quite predictable problems.

In addition to consulting breeders and breed books such as this one (which understandably have a positive breed bias), seek out as many pet owners with your breed you can find. Good points are obvious. What you want to find out are the breed-specific *problems*, so you can nip them in the bud. In particular, you should talk to owners with *adolescent* dogs and make a list of all anticipated problems. Most important, *test drive* at least half a dozen adolescent and adult dogs of your breed yourself. An eight-week-old puppy is deceptively easy to handle, but she will acquire adult size, speed and strength in just four months, so you should learn now what to prepare for.

Puppy and pet dog training classes offer a convenient venue to locate pet owners and observe dogs in action. For a list of suitable trainers in your area, contact the Association of Pet Dog Trainers (see Chapter 13). You may also begin your basic owner training by observing other owners in class. Watch as many classes and test drive as many dogs as possible. Select an upbeat, dog-friendly, people-friendly, fun-and-games, puppydog pet training class to learn the ropes. Also, watch training videos and read training books (see Chapter 12). You must find out what to do and how to do it *before* you have to do it.

Principles of Training

Most people think training comprises teaching the dog to do things such as sit, speak and roll over, but even a four-week-old pup knows how to do these things already. Instead, the first step in training involves teaching the dog human words for each dog behavior and activity and for each aspect of the dog's environment. That way you, the owner, can more easily participate in the dog's domestic education by directing him to perform specific actions appropriately, that is, at the right time, in the right place, and so on. Training opens communication channels, enabling an educated dog to at least understand the owner's requests.

In addition to teaching a dog *what* we want her to do, it is also necessary to teach her *why* she should do what we ask. Indeed, 95 percent of training revolves around motivating the dog *to want to do* what we want. Dogs often understand what their owners want; they just don't see the point of doing it—especially when the owner's repetitively boring and seemingly senseless instructions are totally at odds with much more pressing and exciting doggy distractions. It is not so much the dog who is being stubborn or dominant; rather, it is the owner who has failed to acknowledge the dog's needs and feelings and to approach training from the dog's point of view.

The Meaning of Instructions

The secret to successful training is learning how to use training lures to predict or prompt specific behaviors—to coax the dog to do what you want *when* you want. Any highly valued object (such as a treat or toy) may be used as a lure, which the dog will follow with his eyes and nose. Moving the lure in specific ways entices the dog to move his nose, head and entire body in specific ways. In fact, by learning the art of manipulating various lures, it is possible to teach the dog to assume virtually any body position and perform any action. Once you have control over the expression of the dog's behaviors and can elicit any body position or behavior at will, you can easily teach the dog to perform on request.

Tell your dog what you want him to do, use a lure to entice him to respond correctly, then profusely praise

Teach your dog words for each activity he needs to know, like down.

and maybe reward him once he performs the desired action. For example, verbally request "Fido, sit!" while you move a squeaky toy upwards and backwards over the dog's muzzle (lure-movement and hand signal), smile knowingly as he looks up (to follow the lure) and sits down (as a result of canine anatomical engineering), then praise him to distraction ("Gooood Fido!"). Squeak the toy, offer a training treat and give your dog and yourself a pat on the back.

Being able to elicit desired responses over and over enables the owner to reward the dog over and over. Consequently, the dog begins to think training is fun. For example, the more the dog is rewarded for sitting, the more she enjoys sitting. Eventually the dog comes to realize that, whereas most sitting is appreciated, sitting immediately upon request usually prompts especially enthusiastic praise and a slew of high-level rewards. The dog begins to sit on cue much of the time, showing that she is starting to grasp the meaning of the owner's verbal request and hand signal.

Why Comply?

Most dogs enjoy initial lure/reward training and are only too happy to comply with their owners' wishes. Unfortunately, repetitive drilling without appreciative feedback tends to diminish the dog's enthusiasm until he eventually fails to see the point of complying anymore. Moreover, as the dog approaches adolescence he becomes more easily distracted as he develops other interests. Lengthy sessions with repetitive exercises tend to bore and demotivate both parties. If it's not fun, the owner doesn't do it and neither does the dog.

Integrate training into your dog's life: The greater number of training sessions each day and the *shorter* they are, the more willingly compliant your dog will become. Make sure to have a short (just a few seconds) training interlude before every enjoyable canine activity. For example, ask your dog to sit to greet people, to sit before you throw his Frisbee, and to sit for his supper. Really, sitting is no different from a canine "please." Also, include numerous short training interludes during every enjoyable canine pastime, for example, when playing with the dog or when he is running in the park. In this fashion, doggy distractions may be effectively converted into rewards for training. Just as all games have rules, fun becomes training . . . and training becomes fun.

Eventually, rewards actually become unnecessary to continue motivating your dog. If trained with consideration and kindness, performing the desired behaviors will become self-rewarding and, in a sense, your dog will motivate himself. Just as it is not necessary to reward a human companion during an enjoyable walk in the park, or following a game of tennis, it is hardly necessary to reward our best friend—the dog—for walking by our side or while playing fetch. Human

company during enjoyable activities is reward enough for most dogs.

Even though your dog has become self-motivating, it's still good to praise and pet him a lot and offer rewards once in a while, especially for a good job well done. And if for no other reason, praising and rewarding others is good for the human heart.

To train your dog, you need gentle hands, a loving heart and a good attitude.

Punishment

Without a doubt, lure/reward training is by far the best way to teach: Entice your dog to do what you want and then reward him for doing so. Unfortunately, a human shortcoming is to take the good for granted and to moan and groan at the bad. Specifically, the dog's many good behaviors are ignored while the owner focuses on punishing the dog for making mistakes. In extreme cases, instruction is *limited* to punishing mistakes made by a trainee dog, child, employee or husband, even though it has been proven punishment training is notoriously inefficient and ineffective and is decidedly unfriendly and combative. It teaches the dog that training is a drag, almost as quickly as it teaches the dog to dislike his trainer. Why treat our best friends like our worst enemies?

Punishment training is also much more laborious and time consuming. Whereas it takes only a finite amount of time to teach a dog what to chew, for example, it takes much, much longer to punish the dog for each and every mistake. Remember, *there is only one right way!* So why not teach that right way from the outset?!

To make matters worse, punishment training causes severe lapses in the dog's reliability. Since it is obviously impossible to punish the dog each and every time she misbehaves, the dog quickly learns to distinguish between those times when she must comply (so as to avoid impending punishment) and those times when she need not comply, because punishment is impossible. Such times include when the dog is off leash and only six feet away, when the owner is otherwise engaged (talking to a friend, watching television, taking a shower, tending to the baby or chatting on the telephone), or when the dog is left at home alone.

Instances of misbehavior will be numerous when the owner is away, because even when the dog complied in the owner's looming presence, he did so unwillingly. The dog was forced to act against his will, rather than moulding his will to want to please. Hence, when the owner is absent, not only does the dog know he need not comply, he simply does not want to. Again, the trainee is not a stubborn vindictive beast, but rather the trainer has failed to teach.

Punishment training invariably creates unpredictable Jekyll and Hyde behavior.

Trainer's Tools

Many training books extol the virtues of a vast array of training paraphernalia and electronic and metallic gizmos, most of which are designed for canine restraint, correction and punishment, rather than for actual facilitation of doggy education. In reality, most effective training tools are not found in stores; they come from within ourselves. In addition to a willing dog, all you really need is a functional human brain, gentle hands, a loving heart and a good attitude.

In terms of equipment, all dogs do require a quality buckle collar to sport dog tags and to attach the leash (for safety and to comply with local leash laws). Hollow chewtoys (like Kongs or sterilized longbones) and a dog bed or collapsible crate are a must for housetraining. Three additional tools are required:

1. specific lures (training treats and toys) to predict and prompt specific desired behaviors;

2. rewards (praise, affection, training treats and toys) to reinforce for the dog what a lot of fun it all is; and

3. knowledge—how to convert the dog's favorite activities and games (potential distractions to training) into "life-rewards," which may be employed to facilitate training.

The most powerful of these is *knowledge*. Education is the key! Watch training classes, participate in training classes, watch videos, read books, enjoy playtraining with your dog, and then your dog will say "Please," and your dog will say "Thank you!"

Housetraining

If dogs were left to their own devices, certainly they would chew, dig and bark for entertainment and then no doubt highlight a few areas of their living space with sprinkles of urine, in much the same way we decorate by hanging pictures. Consequently, when we ask a dog to live with us, we must teach him *where* he may dig and perform his toilet duties, *what* he may chew and *when* he may bark. After all, when left at home alone for many hours, we cannot expect the dog to amuse himself by completing crosswords or watching the soaps on TV!

Also, it would be decidedly unfair to keep the house rules a secret from the dog, and then get angry and punish the poor critter for inevitably transgressing rules he did not even know existed. Remember, without adequate education and guidance, the dog will be forced to establish his own rules—doggy rules—that most probably will be at odds with the owner's view of domestic living.

Since most problems develop during the first few days the dog is at home, prospective dog owners must be certain they are quite clear about the principles of housetraining *before* they get a dog. Early misbehaviors quickly become established as the status quo—

becoming firmly entrenched as hard-to-break bad habits, which set the precedent for years to come. Make sure to teach your dog good habits right from the start. Good habits are just as hard to break as bad ones!

Ideally, when a new dog comes home, try to arrange for someone to be present for as much as possible during the first few days (for adult dogs) or weeks for puppies. With only a little forethought, it is surprisingly easy to find a puppy sitter, such as a retired person, who would be willing to eat from your refrigerator and watch your television while keeping an eye on the newcomer to encourage the dog to play with chewtoys and to ensure he goes outside on a regular basis.

POTTY TRAINING

To teach the dog where to relieve himself:

1. never let him make a single mistake;
2. let him know where you want him to go; and
3. handsomely reward him for doing so: "GOOOOOOOD DOG!!!" liver treat, liver treat, liver treat!

PREVENTING MISTAKES

A single mistake is a training disaster, since it heralds many more in future weeks. And each time the dog soils the house, this further reinforces the dog's unfortunate preference for an indoor, carpeted toilet. *Do not let an unhousetrained dog have full run of the house if you are away from home or cannot pay full attention.* Instead, confine the dog to an area where elimination is appropriate, such as an outdoor run or, better still, a small, comfortable indoor kennel with access to an outdoor run. When confined in this manner, most dogs will naturally housetrain themselves.

If that's not possible, confine the dog to an area, such as a utility room, kitchen, basement or garage, where elimination may not be desired in the long run but as an interim measure it is certainly preferable to doing it all around the house. Use newspaper to cover the floor of the dog's day room. The newspaper may be used to soak up the urine and to wrap up and dispose of the feces. Once your dog develops a preferred spot for eliminating, it is only necessary to cover that part of the floor with newspaper. The smaller papered area may then be moved (only a little each day) towards the door to the outside. Thus the dog will develop the tendency to go to the door when he needs to relieve himself.

Never confine an unhousetrained dog to a crate for long periods. Doing so would force the dog to soil the crate and ruin its usefulness as an aid for housetraining (see the following discussion).

The first few weeks at home are the most important and influential in your dog's life.

TEACHING WHERE

In order to teach your dog where you would like her to do her business, you have to be there to direct the proceedings—an obvious, yet often neglected, fact of life. In order to be there to teach the dog *where* to go, you need to know *when* she needs to go. Indeed, the success of housetraining depends on the owner's ability to predict these times. Certainly, a regular feeding schedule will facilitate prediction somewhat, but there is nothing like "loading the deck" and influencing the timing of the outcome yourself!

Whenever you are at home, make sure the dog is under constant supervision and/or confined to a small area. If already well trained, simply instruct the dog to lie down in his bed or basket. Alternatively, confine the dog to a crate (doggy den) or tie-down (a short, 18-inch lead that can be clipped to an eye hook in the baseboard). Short-term close confinement strongly inhibits urination and defecation, since the dog does not want to soil his sleeping area. Thus, when you release the puppydog each hour, he will definitely need to urinate immediately and defecate every third or fourth hour. Keep the dog confined to his doggy den and take him to his intended toilet area each hour, every hour, and on the hour.

When taking your dog outside, instruct him to sit quietly before opening the door—he will soon learn to sit by the door when he needs to go out!

TEACHING WHY

Being able to predict when the dog needs to go enables the owner to be on the spot to praise and reward the dog. Each hour, hurry the dog to the intended toilet area in the yard, issue the appropriate instruction ("Go pee!" or "Go poop!"), then give the dog three to four minutes to produce. Praise and offer a couple of training treats when successful. The treats are important because many people fail to praise their dogs with feeling . . . and housetraining is hardly the time for understatement. So either loosen up and enthusiastically praise that dog: "Wuzzzer-wuzzer-wuzzer, hoooser good wuffer den? Hoooo went pee for Daddy?" Or say "Good dog!" as best you can and offer the treats for effect.

Following elimination is an ideal time for a spot of playtraining in the yard or house. Also, an empty dog may be allowed greater freedom around the house for the next half hour or so, just as long as you keep an eye out to make sure he does not get into other kinds of mischief. If you are preoccupied and cannot pay full attention, confine the dog to his doggy den once more to enjoy a peaceful snooze or to play with his many chewtoys.

If your dog does not eliminate within the allotted time outside—no biggie! Back to his doggy den, and then try again after another hour.

As I own large dogs, I always feel more relaxed walking an empty dog, knowing that I will not need to finish our stroll weighted down with bags of feces! Beware of falling into the trap of walking the dog to get it to eliminate. The good ol' dog walk is such an enormous highlight in the dog's life that it represents the single biggest potential reward in domestic dogdom. However, when in a hurry, or during inclement weather, many owners abruptly terminate the walk the moment the dog has done its business. This, in effect, severely punishes the dog for doing the right thing, in the right place at the right time. Consequently, many dogs become strongly inhibited from eliminating outdoors because they know it will signal an abrupt end to an otherwise thoroughly enjoyable walk.

Instead, instruct the dog to relieve himself in the yard prior to going for a walk. If you follow the above instructions, most dogs soon learn to eliminate on cue. As soon as the dog eliminates, praise (and offer a treat or two)—"Good dog! Let's go walkies!" Use the walk as a reward for eliminating in the yard. If the dog does not go, put him back in his doggy den and think about a walk later on. You will find with a "No feces–no walk" policy, your dog will become one of the fastest defecators in the business.

If you do not have a back yard, instruct the dog to eliminate right outside your front door prior to the walk. Not only will this facilitate clean up and disposal of the feces in your own trash can but, also, the walk may again be used as a colossal reward.

Chewing and Barking

Short-term close confinement also teaches the dog that occasional quiet moments are a reality of domestic living. Your puppydog is extremely impressionable during his first few weeks at home. Regular confinement at this time soon exerts a calming influence over the dog's personality. Remember, once the dog is housetrained and calmer, there will be a whole lifetime ahead for the dog to enjoy full run of the house and garden. On the other hand, by letting the newcomer have unrestricted access to the entire household and allowing him to run willy-nilly, he will most certainly develop a bunch of behavior problems in short order, no doubt necessitating confinement later in life. It would not be fair to remedially restrain and confine a dog you have trained, through neglect, to run free.

When confining the dog, make sure he always has an impressive array of suitable chewtoys. Kongs and sterilized longbones (both readily available from pet stores) make the best chewtoys, since they are hollow and may be stuffed with treats to heighten the dog's interest. For example, by stuffing the little hole at the top of a Kong with a small piece of freeze-dried liver, the dog will not want to leave it alone.

Remember, treats do not have to be junk food and they certainly should not represent extra calories. Rather, treats should be part of each dog's regular daily diet:

Make sure your puppy has suitable chewtoys.

Some food may be served in the dog's bowl for breakfast and dinner, some food may be used as training treats, and some food may be used for stuffing chewtoys. I regularly stuff my dogs' many Kongs with different shaped biscuits and kibble. The kibble seems to fall out fairly easily, as do the oval-shaped biscuits, thus rewarding the dog instantaneously for checking out the chewtoys. The bone-shaped biscuits fall out after a while, rewarding the dog for worrying at the chewtoy. But the triangular biscuits never come out. They remain inside the Kong as lures, maintaining the dog's fascination with its chewtoy. To further focus the dog's interest, I always make sure to flavor the triangular biscuits by rubbing them with a little cheese or freeze-dried liver.

If stuffed chewtoys are reserved especially for times the dog is confined, the puppy-dog will soon learn to enjoy quiet moments in her doggy den and she will quickly develop a chewtoy habit—a good habit! This is a simple *passive training* process; all the owner has to do is set up the situation and the dog all but trains herself—easy and effective. Even when the dog is given run of the house, her first inclination will be to indulge her rewarding chewtoy habit rather than destroying less-attractive household articles, such as curtains, carpets, chairs and compact disks. Similarly, a chewtoy chewer will be less inclined to scratch and chew herself excessively. Also, if the dog busies herself as a recreational chewer, she will be less inclined to develop into a recreational barker or digger when left at home alone.

Stuff a number of chewtoys whenever the dog is left confined and remove the extra-special-tasting treats when you return. Your dog will now amuse himself with his chewtoys before falling asleep and then resume playing with his chewtoys when he expects you to return. Since most owner-absent misbehavior happens right after you leave and right before your expected return, your puppydog will now be conveniently preoccupied with his chewtoys at these times.

To teach come, call your dog, open your arms as a welcoming signal, wave a toy or a treat and praise for every step in your direction.

Come and Sit

Most puppies will happily approach virtually anyone, whether called or not; that is, until they collide with adolescence and develop other more important doggy interests, such as sniffing a multiplicity of exquisite odors on the grass. Your mission, Mr. and/or Ms. Owner, is to teach and reward the pup for coming reliably, willingly and happily when called—and you have just three months to get it done. Unless adequately reinforced, your puppy's tendency to approach people will self-destruct by adolescence.

Call your dog ("Fido, come!"), open your arms (and maybe squat down) as a welcoming signal, waggle a treat or toy as a lure, and reward the puppydog when he comes running. Do not wait to praise the dog until he reaches you—he may come 95 percent of the way and then run off after some distraction. Instead, praise the dog's *first* step towards you and continue praising enthusiastically for *every* step he takes in your direction.

When the rapidly approaching puppy dog is three lengths away from impact, instruct him to sit ("Fido, sit!") and hold the lure in front of you in an outstretched hand to prevent him from hitting you midchest and knocking you flat on your back! As Fido decelerates to nose the lure, move the treat upwards and backwards just over his muzzle with an upwards motion of your extended arm (palm-upwards). As the dog looks up to follow the lure, he will sit down (if he jumps up, you are holding the lure too high). Praise the dog for sitting. Move backwards and call him again. Repeat this many times over, always praising when Fido comes and sits; on occasion, reward him.

For the first couple of trials, use a training treat both as a lure to entice the dog to come and sit and as a reward for doing so. Thereafter, try to use different items as lures and rewards. For example, lure the dog with a Kong or Frisbee but reward her with a food treat. Or lure the dog with a food treat but pat her and throw a tennis ball as a reward. After just a few repetitions, dispense with the lures and rewards; the dog will begin to respond willingly to your verbal requests and hand signals just for the prospect of praise from your heart and affection from your hands.

Instruct every family member, friend and visitor how to get the dog to come and sit. Invite people over for a series of pooch parties; do not keep the pup a secret— let other people enjoy this puppy, and let the pup enjoy other people. Puppydog parties are not only fun, they easily attract a lot of people to help *you* train *your* dog. Unless you teach your dog *how* to meet people, that is, to sit for greetings, no doubt the dog will resort to jumping up. Then you and the visitors will get annoyed, and the dog will be punished. This is not fair. *Send out those invitations for puppy parties and teach your dog to be mannerly and socially acceptable.*

Even though your dog quickly masters obedient recalls in the house, his reliability may falter when playing in the back yard or local park. Ironically, it is *the owner* who has unintentionally trained the dog *not* to respond in these instances. By allowing the dog to play and run around and otherwise have a good time, but then to call the dog to put him on leash to take him home, the dog quickly learns playing is fun but training is a drag. Thus, playing in the park becomes a severe distraction, which works against training. Bad news!

Instead, whether playing with the dog off leash or on leash, request him to come at frequent intervals— say, every minute or so. On most occasions, praise and pet the dog for a few seconds while he is sitting, then tell him to go play again. For especially fast recalls, offer a couple of training treats and take the time to praise and pet the dog enthusiastically before releasing him. The dog will learn that coming when called is not necessarily the end of the play session, and neither is it the end of the world; rather, it signals an enjoyable, quality time-out with the owner before resuming play once more. In fact, playing in the park now becomes a very effective life-reward, which works to facilitate training by reinforcing each obedient and timely recall. Good news!

Sit, Down, Stand and Rollover

Teaching the dog a variety of body positions is easy for owner and dog, impressive for spectators and extremely useful for all. Using lure-reward techniques, it is possible to train several positions at once to verbal commands or hand signals (which impress the socks off onlookers).

Sit and *down*—the two control commands—prevent or resolve nearly a hundred behavior problems. For example, if the dog happily and obediently sits or lies down when requested, he cannot jump on visitors, dash out the front door, run around and chase its tail, pester other dogs, harass cats or annoy family, friends or strangers. Additionally, "sit" or "down" are better emergency commands for off-leash control.

It is easier to teach and maintain a reliable sit than maintain a reliable recall. *Sit* is the purest and simplest of commands—either the dog is sitting or he is not. If there is any change of circumstances or potential danger in the park, for example, simply instruct the dog to sit. If he sits, you have a number of options: allow the dog to resume playing when he is safe; walk up and put the dog on leash, or call the dog. The dog will be much more likely to come when called if he has already acknowledged his compliance by sitting. If the dog does not sit in the park—train him to!

Stand and *rollover-stay* are the two positions for examining the dog. Your veterinarian will love you to distraction if you take a little time to teach the dog to stand still and roll over and play possum. Also, your vet bills will be smaller. The rollover-stay is an especially useful command and is really just a variation of the down-stay: whereas the dog lies prone in the traditional down, she lies supine in the rollover-stay.

As with teaching come and sit, the training techniques to teach the dog to assume all other body positions on cue are user-friendly and dog-friendly. Simply give the appropriate request, lure the dog into the desired body position using a training treat or toy and then *praise* (and maybe reward) the dog as soon as he complies. Try not to touch the dog to get him to respond. If you teach the dog by guiding him into position, the dog will quickly learn that rump-pressure means sit, for example, but as yet you still have no control over your dog if he is just six feet away. It will still be necessary to teach the dog to sit on request. So do not make training a time-consuming two-step process; instead, teach the dog to sit to a verbal request or hand signal from the outset. Once the dog sits willingly when requested, by all means use your hands to pet the dog when he does so.

To teach *down* when the dog is already sitting, say "Fido, down!," hold the lure in one hand (palm down) and lower that hand to the floor between the dog's forepaws. As the dog lowers his head to follow the lure, slowly move the lure away from the dog just a fraction (in front of his paws). The dog will lie down as he stretches his nose forward to follow the lure. Praise the dog when he does so. If the dog stands up, you pulled the lure away too far and too quickly.

When teaching the dog to lie down from the standing position, say "down" and lower the lure to the floor as before. Once the dog has lowered his forequarters and assumed a play bow, gently and slowly move the lure *towards* the dog between his forelegs. Praise the dog as soon as his rear end plops down.

After just a couple of trials it will be possible to alternate sits and downs and have the dog energetically perform doggy push-ups. Praise the dog a lot, and after half a dozen or so push-ups reward the dog with a training treat or toy. You will notice the more energetically you move your arm—upwards (palm up) to get the dog to sit, and downwards (palm down) to get the dog to lie down—the more energetically the dog responds to your requests. Now try training the dog in silence and you will notice he has also learned to respond to hand signals. Yeah! Not too shabby for the first session.

To teach *stand* from the sitting position, say "Fido, stand," slowly move the lure half a dog-length away from the dog's nose, keeping it at nose level, and praise the dog as he stands to follow the lure. As soon

Using a food lure to teach sit, down and stand. 1) "Phoenix, Sit." 2) Hand palm upwards, move up and back over dog's muzzle. 3) "Good sit, Phoenix!" 4) "Phoenix, down." 5) Hand palm downwards, move lure down to lie between dog's forepaws. 6) "Phoenix, off. Good down, Phoenix!" 7) "Phoenix, sit!" 8) Palm upwards, move lure up and back, keeping it close to dog's muzzle. 9) "Good sit, Phoenix!"

10) "Phoenix, stand!" 11) Move lure away from dog at nose height, then lower it a tad. 12) "Phoenix, off! Good stand, Phoenix!" 13) "Phoenix, down!" 14) Hand palm downwards, move lure down to lie between dog's forepaws. 15) "Phoenix, off! Good down-stay, Phoenix!" 16) "Phoenix, stand!" 17) Move lure away from dog's muzzle up to nose height. 18) "Phoenix, off! Good stand-stay, Phoenix. Now we'll make the vet and groomer happy!"

Enjoying Your
Dog

as the dog stands, lower the lure to just beneath the dog's chin to entice him to look down; otherwise he will stand and then sit immediately. To prompt the dog to stand from the down position, move the lure half a dog-length upwards and away from the dog, holding the lure at standing nose height from the floor.

Teaching *rollover* is best started from the down position, with the dog lying on one side, or at least with both hind legs stretched out on the same side. Say "Fido, bang!" and move the lure backwards and alongside the dog's muzzle to its elbow (on the side of its outstretched hind legs). Once the dog looks to the side and backwards, very slowly move the lure upwards to the dog's shoulder and backbone. Tickling the dog in the goolies (groin area) often invokes a reflex-raising of the hind leg as an appeasement gesture, which facilitates the tendency to roll over. If you move the lure too quickly and the dog jumps into the standing position, have patience and start again. As soon as the dog rolls onto its back, keep the lure stationary and mesmerize the dog with a relaxing tummy rub.

To teach *rollover-stay* when the dog is standing or moving, say "Fido, bang!" and give the appropriate hand signal (with index finger pointed and thumb cocked in true Sam Spade fashion), then in one fluid movement lure him to first lie down and then rollover-stay as above.

Teaching the dog to *stay* in each of the above four positions becomes a piece of cake after first teaching the dog not to worry at the toy or treat training lure. This is best accomplished by hand feeding dinner kibble. Hold a piece of kibble firmly in your hand and softly instruct "Off!" Ignore any licking and slobbering *for however long the dog worries at the treat*, but say "Take it!" and offer the kibble *the instant* the dog breaks contact with his muzzle. Repeat this a few times, and then up the ante and insist the dog remove his muzzle for one whole second before offering the kibble. Then progressively refine your criteria and have the dog not touch your hand (or treat) for longer and longer periods on each trial, such as for two seconds, four seconds, then six, ten, fifteen, twenty, thirty seconds and so on. The dog soon learns: (1) worrying at the treat never gets results, whereas (2) noncontact is often rewarded after a variable time lapse.

Teaching *"Off!"* has many useful applications in its own right. Additionally, instructing the dog not to touch a training lure often produces spontaneous and magical stays. Request the dog to stand-stay, for example, and not to touch the lure. At first set your sights on a short two-second stay before rewarding the dog. (Remember, every long journey begins with a single step.) However, on subsequent trials, gradually and progressively increase the length of stay required to receive a reward. In no time at all your dog will stand calmly for a minute or so.

Relevancy Training

Once you have taught the dog what you expect her to do when requested to come, sit, lie down, stand, rollover and stay, the time is right to teach the dog *why* she should comply with your wishes. The secret is to have many (*many*) extremely short training interludes (two to five seconds each) at numerous (*numerous*) times during the course of the dog's day. Especially work with the dog immediately *before* the dog's good times and *during* the dog's good times. For example, ask your dog to sit and/or lie down each time before opening doors, serving meals, offering treats and tummy rubs; ask the dog to perform a few controlled doggy push-ups before letting her off-leash or throwing a tennis ball; and perhaps request the dog to sit-down-sit-stand-down-stand-rollover before inviting her to cuddle on the couch.

Similarly, request the dog to sit many times during play or on walks, and in no time at all the dog will be only too pleased to follow your instructions because he has learned that a compliant response heralds all sorts of goodies. Basically all you are trying to teach the dog is how to say please: "Please throw the tennis ball. Please may I snuggle on the couch."

Remember, whereas it is important to keep training interludes short, it is equally important to have many short sessions each and every day. The shortest (and most useful) session comprises asking the dog to sit and then go play during a play session. When trained this way, your dog will soon associate training with good times. In fact, the dog may be unable to distinguish between training and good times and, indeed, there should be no distinction. The warped concept that training involves forcing the dog to comply and/or dominating his will is totally at odds with the picture of a truly well-trained dog. In reality, enjoying a game of training with a dog is no different from enjoying a game of backgammon or tennis with a friend; and walking with a dog should be no different from strolling with buddies on the golf course.

Walk by Your Side

Many people attempt to teach a dog to heel by putting him on a leash and physically correcting the dog when he makes mistakes. There are a number of things seriously wrong with this approach, the first being that most people do not want precision heeling; rather, they simply want the dog to follow or walk by their side. Second, when physically restrained during "training," even though the dog may grudgingly mope by your side when "handcuffed" on leash, let's see what happens when he is off leash. History! The dog is in the next county because he never enjoyed walking with you on leash and you have no control over him off leash. So let's just teach the dog off leash from the outset to *want* to walk with us. Third, if the dog has not been trained to heel, it is a trifle hasty to think about punishing the poor dog for making mistakes and breaking heeling rules he didn't even know existed. This is simply not fair! Surely, if the dog had been adequately taught how to heel, he would seldom make mistakes and hence there would be no need to correct the dog. Remember, each mistake and each correction (punishment) advertise the trainer's inadequacy, not the dog's. The dog is not stubborn, he is not stupid and he is not bad. Even if he were, he would still require training, so let's train him properly.

Let's teach the dog to *enjoy* following us and to *want* to walk by our side offleash. Then it will be easier to teach high-precision off-leash heeling patterns if desired. After attaching the leash for safety on outdoor walks, but before going anywhere, it is necessary to teach the dog specifically not to pull. Now it will be much easier to teach on-leash walking and heeling because the dog already wants to walk with you, he is familiar with the desired walking and heeling positions and he knows not to pull.

FOLLOWING

Start by training your dog to follow you. Many puppies will follow if you simply walk away from them and maybe click your fingers or chuckle. Adult dogs may require additional enticement to stimulate them to follow, such as a training lure or, at the very least, a lively trainer. To teach the dog to follow: (1) keep walking and (2) walk away from the dog. If the dog attempts to lead or lag, change pace; slow down if the dog forges too far ahead, but speed up if he lags too far behind. Say "Steady!" or "Easy!" each time before you slow down and "Quickly!" or "Hustle!" each time before you speed up, and the dog will learn to change pace on cue. If the dog lags or leads too far, or if he wanders right or left, simply walk quickly in the opposite direction and maybe even run away from the dog and hide.

Practicing is a lot of fun; you can set up a course in your home, yard or park to do this. Indoors, entice the dog to follow upstairs, into a bedroom, into the bathroom, downstairs, around the living room couch, zigzagging between dining room chairs and into the kitchen for dinner. Outdoors, get the dog to follow around park benches, trees, shrubs and along walkways and lines in the grass. (For safety outdoors, it is advisable to attach a long line on the dog, but never exert corrective tension on the line.)

Remember, following has a lot to do with attitude—
your attitude! Most probably your dog will *not* want to
follow Mr. Grumpy Troll with the personality of wilted
lettuce. Lighten up—walk with a jaunty step, whistle a
happy tune, sing, skip and tell jokes to your dog and he
will be right there by your side.

BY YOUR SIDE

It is smart to train the dog to walk close on one side or
the other—either side will do, your choice. When walking, jogging or cycling, it is generally bad news to have
the dog suddenly cut in front of you. In fact, I train my
dogs to walk "By my side" and "Other side"—both very
useful instructions. It is possible to position the dog
fairly accurately by looking to the appropriate side and
clicking your fingers or slapping your thigh on that
side. A precise positioning may be attained by holding
a training lure, such as a chewtoy, tennis ball, or food
treat. Stop and stand still several times throughout the
walk, just as you would when window shopping or
meeting a friend. Use the lure to make sure the dog
slows down and stays close whenever you stop.

When teaching the dog to heel, we generally want
her to sit in heel position when we stop. Teach heel

*Using a toy to teach sit-heel-sit sequences: 1) "Phoenix, heel!" Standing still, move lure up and back
over dog's muzzle.... 2) To position dog sitting in heel position on your left side. 3) "Phoenix, heel!"
wagging lure in left hand. Change lure to right hand in preparation for sit signal.*

position at the standstill and the dog will learn that the default heel position is sitting by your side (left or right—your choice, unless you wish to compete in obedience trials, in which case the dog must heel on the left).

Several times a day, stand up and call your dog to come and sit in heel position—"Fido, heel!" For example, instruct the dog to come to heel each time there are commercials on TV, or each time you turn a page of a novel, and the dog will get it in a single evening.

Practice straight-line heeling and turns separately. With the dog sitting at heel, teach him to turn in place. After each quarter-turn, half-turn or full turn in place, lure the dog to sit at heel. Now it's time for short straight-line heeling sequences, no more than a few steps at a time. Always think of heeling in terms of Sit-Heel-Sit sequences—start and end with the dog in position and do your best to keep him there when moving. Progressively increase the number of steps in each sequence. When the dog remains close for 20 yards of straight-line heeling, it is time to add a few turns and then sign up for a happy-heeling obedience class to get some advice from the experts.

4) Use hand signal only to lure dog to sit as you stop. Eventually, dog will sit automatically at heel whenever you stop. 5) "Good dog!"

No Pulling on Leash

You can start teaching your dog not to pull on leash anywhere—in front of the television or outdoors—but regardless of location, you must not take a single step with tension in the leash. For a reason known only to dogs, even just a couple of paces of pulling on leash is intrinsically motivating and diabolically rewarding. Instead, attach the leash to the dog's collar, grasp the other end firmly with both hands held close to your chest, and stand still—do not budge an inch. Have somebody watch you with a stopwatch to time your progress, or else you will never believe this will work and so you will not even try the exercise, and your shoulder and the dog's neck will be traumatized for years to come.

Stand still and wait for the dog to stop pulling, and to sit and/or lie down. All dogs stop pulling and sit eventually. Most take only a couple of minutes; the all-time record is 22 ⅕ minutes. Time how long it takes. Gently praise the dog when he stops pulling, and as soon as he sits, enthusiastically praise the dog and take just one step forwards, then immediately stand still. This single step usually demonstrates the ballistic reinforcing nature of pulling on leash; most dogs explode to the end of the leash, so be prepared for the strain. Stand firm and wait for the dog to sit again. Repeat this half a dozen times and you will probably notice a progressive reduction in the force of the dog's one-step explosions and a radical reduction in the time it takes for the dog to sit each time.

As the dog learns "Sit we go" and "Pull we stop," she will begin to walk forward calmly with each single step and automatically sit when you stop. Now try two steps before you stop. Wooooooo! Scary! When the dog has mastered two steps at a time, try for three. After each success, progressively increase the number of steps in the sequence: try four steps and then six, eight, ten and twenty steps before stopping. Congratulations! You are now walking the dog on leash.

Whenever walking with the dog (off leash or on leash), make sure you stop periodically to practice a few position commands and stays before instructing the dog to "Walk on!" (Remember, you want the dog to be compliant everywhere, not just in the kitchen when his dinner is at hand.) For example, stopping every 25 yards to briefly train the dog amounts to over 200 training interludes within a single three-mile stroll. And each training session is in a different location. You will not believe the improvement within just the first mile of the first walk.

To put it another way, integrating training into a walk offers 200 separate opportunities to use the continuance of the walk as a reward to reinforce the dog's education. Moreover, some training interludes may comprise continuing education for the dog's walking skills: Alternate short periods of the dog walking calmly by your side with periods when the dog is allowed to sniff and investigate the environment. Now sniffing odors on the grass and meeting other dogs become rewards which reinforce the dog's calm and mannerly demeanor. Good Lord! Whatever next? Many enjoyable walks together of course. Happy trails!

THE IMPORTANCE OF TRICKS

Nothing will improve a dog's quality of life better than having a few tricks under its belt. Teaching any trick expands the dog's vocabulary, which facilitates communication and improves the owner's control. Also, specific tricks help prevent and resolve specific behavior problems. For example, by teaching the dog to fetch his toys, the dog learns carrying a toy makes the owner happy and, therefore, will be more likely to chew his toy than other inappropriate items.

More important, teaching tricks prompts owners to lighten up and train with a sunny disposition. Really, tricks should be no different from any other behaviors we put on cue. But they are. When teaching tricks, owners have a much sweeter attitude, which in turn motivates the dog and improves her willingness to comply. The dog feels tricks are a blast, but formal commands are a drag. In fact, tricks are so enjoyable, they may be used as rewards in training by asking the dog to come, sit and down-stay and then rollover for a tummy rub. Go on, try it: Crack a smile and even giggle when the dog promptly and willingly lies down and stays.

Most important, performing tricks prompts onlookers to smile and giggle. Many people are scared of dogs, especially large ones. And nothing can be more off-putting for a dog than to be constantly confronted by strangers who don't like him because of his size or the way he looks. Uneasy people put the dog on edge, causing him to back off and bark, only frightening people all the more. And so a vicious circle develops, with the people's fear fueling the dog's fear *and vice versa*. Instead, tie a pink ribbon to your dog's collar and practice all sorts of tricks on walks and in the park, and you will be pleasantly amazed how it changes people's attitudes toward your friendly dog. The dog's repertoire of tricks is limited only by the trainer's imagination. Below I have described three of my favorites:

SPEAK AND SHUSH

The training sequence involved in teaching a dog to bark on request is no different from that used when training any behavior on cue: request—lure—response—reward. As always, the secret of success lies in finding an effective lure. If the dog always barks at the doorbell, for example, say "Rover, speak!", have an accomplice ring the doorbell, then reward the dog for barking. After a few woofs, ask Rover to "Shush!", waggle a food treat under his nose (to entice him to sniff and thus to shush), praise him when quiet and eventually offer the treat as a reward. Alternate "Speak" and "Shush," progressively increasing the length of shush-time between each barking bout.

PLAYBOW

With the dog standing, say "Bow!" and lower the food lure (palm upwards) to rest between the dog's forepaws. Praise as the dog lowers her forequarters and sternum to the ground (as when teaching the down), but then lure the dog to stand and offer the treat. On successive trials, gradually increase the length of time the dog is required to remain in the playbow posture in order to gain a food reward. If the dog's rear end collapses into a down, say nothing and offer no reward; simply start over.

BE A BEAR

With the dog sitting backed into a corner to prevent him from toppling over backwards, say "Be a Bear!" With bent paw and palm down, raise a lure upwards and backwards along the top of the dog's muzzle. Praise the dog when he sits up on his haunches and offer the treat as a reward. To prevent the dog from standing on his hind legs, keep the lure closer to the dog's muzzle. On each trial, progressively increase the length of time the dog is required to sit up to receive a food reward. Since lure/reward training is so easy, teach the dog to stand and walk on his hind legs as well!

Teaching "Be a Bear"

chapter 9

Getting

Active

with your Dog

by Bardi McLennan

Once you and your dog have graduated from basic obedience training and are beginning to work together as a team, you can take part in the growing world of dog activities. There are so many fun things to do with your dog! Just remember, people and dogs don't always learn at the same pace, so don't be upset if you (or your dog) need more than two basic training courses before your team becomes operational. Even smart dogs don't go straight to college from kindergarten!

Just as there are events geared to certain types of dogs, so there are ones that are more appealing to certain types of people. In some activities, you give the commands and your dog does the work (upland game hunting is one example), while in others, such as agility, you'll both get a workout. You may want to aim for prestigious titles to add to your dog's name, or you may want nothing more than the sheer enjoyment of being around other people and their dogs. Passive or active, participation has its own rewards.

Consider your dog's physical capabilities when looking into any of the canine activities. It's easy to see that a Basset Hound is not built for the racetrack, nor would a Chihuahua be the breed of choice for pulling a sled. A loyal dog will attempt almost anything you ask him to do, so it is up to you to know your dog's limitations. A dog must be physically sound in order to compete at any level in athletic activities, and being mentally sound is a definite plus. Advanced age, however, may not be a deterrent. Many dogs still hunt and herd at ten or twelve years of age. It's entirely possible for dogs to be "fit at 50." Take your dog for a checkup, explain to your vet the type of activity you have in mind and be guided by his or her findings.

All dogs seem to love playing flyball.

You needn't be restricted to breed-specific sports if it's only fun you're after. Certain AKC activities are limited to designated breeds; however, as each new trial, test or sport has grown in popularity, so has the variety of breeds encouraged to participate at a fun level.

But don't shortchange your fun, or that of your dog, by thinking only of the basic function of her breed. Once a dog has learned how to learn, she can be taught to do just about anything as long as the size of the dog is right for the job and you both think it is fun and rewarding. In other words, you are a team.

To get involved in any of the activities detailed in this chapter, look for the names and addresses of the organizations that sponsor them in Chapter 13. You can also ask your breeder or a local dog trainer for contacts.

You can compete in obedience trials with a well trained dog.

Official American Kennel Club Activities

The following tests and trials are some of the events sanctioned by the AKC and sponsored by various dog clubs. Your dog's expertise will be rewarded with impressive titles. You can participate just for fun, or be competitive and go for those awards.

OBEDIENCE

Training classes begin with pups as young as three months of age in kindergarten puppy training, then advance to pre-novice (all exercises on lead) and go on to novice, which is where you'll start off-lead work. In obedience classes dogs learn to sit, stay, heel and come through a variety of exercises. Once you've got the basics down, you can enter obedience trials and work toward earning your dog's first degree, a C.D. (Companion Dog).

The next level is called "Open," in which jumps and retrieves perk up the dog's interest. Passing grades in competition at this level earn a C.D.X. (Companion Dog Excellent). Beyond that lies the goal of the most ambitious—Utility (U.D. and even U.D.X. or OTCh, an Obedience Champion).

AGILITY

All dogs can participate in the latest canine sport to have gained worldwide popularity for its fun and excitement, agility. It began in England as a canine version of horse show-jumping, but because dogs are more agile and able to perform on verbal commands, extra feats were added such as climbing, balancing and racing through tunnels or in and out of weave poles.

Many of the obstacles (regulation or homemade) can be set up in your own backyard. If the agility bug bites, you could end up in international competition!

For starters, your dog should be obedience trained, even though, in the beginning, the lessons may all be taught on lead. Once the dog understands the commands (and you do, too), it's as easy as guiding the dog over a prescribed course, one obstacle at a time. In competition, the race is against the clock, so wear your running shoes! The dog starts with 200 points and the judge deducts for infractions and misadventures along the way.

All dogs seem to love agility and respond to it as if they were being turned loose in a playground paradise. Your dog's enthusiasm will be contagious; agility turns into great fun for dog and owner.

FIELD TRIALS AND HUNTING TESTS

There are field trials and hunting tests for the sporting breeds—retrievers, spaniels and pointing breeds, and for some hounds—Bassets, Beagles and Dachshunds. Field trials are competitive events that test a dog's ability to perform the functions for which she was bred. Hunting tests, which are open to retrievers,

---

TITLES AWARDED BY THE AKC

Conformation: Ch. (Champion)

Obedience: CD (Companion Dog); CDX (Companion Dog Excellent); UD (Utility Dog); UDX (Utility Dog Excellent); OTCh. (Obedience Trial Champion)

Field: JH (Junior Hunter); SH (Senior Hunter); MH (Master Hunter); AFCh. (Amateur Field Champion); FCh. (Field Champion)

Lure Coursing: JC (Junior Courser); SC (Senior Courser)

Herding: HT (Herding Tested); PT (Pre-Trial Tested); HS (Herding Started); HI (Herding Intermediate); HX (Herding Excellent); HCh. (Herding Champion)

Tracking: TD (Tracking Dog); TDX (Tracking Dog Excellent)

Agility: NAD (Novice Agility); OAD (Open Agility); ADX (Agility Excellent); MAX (Master Agility)

Earthdog Tests: JE (Junior Earthdog); SE (Senior Earthdog); ME (Master Earthdog)

Canine Good Citizen: CGC

Combination: DC (Dual Champion—Ch. and Fch.); TC (Triple Champion—Ch., Fch., and OTCh.)

spaniels and pointing breeds only, are noncompetitive
and are a means of judging the dog's ability as well as
that of the handler.

Hunting is a very large and complex part of canine
sports, and if you own one of the breeds that hunts, the
events are a great treat for your dog and you. He gets
to do what he was bred for, and you get to work with
him and watch him do it. You'll be proud of and
amazed at what your dog can do.

Fortunately, the AKC publishes a series of booklets on
these events, which outline the rules and regulations
and include a glossary of the sometimes complicated
terms. The AKC also publishes newsletters for field tri-
alers and hunting test enthusiasts. The United Kennel
Club (UKC) also has informative materials for the
hunter and his dog.

*Retrievers and
other sporting
breeds get to do
what they're
bred to in hunt-
ing tests.*

HERDING TESTS AND TRIALS

Herding, like hunting, dates
back to the first known uses man
made of dogs. The interest in
herding today is widespread,
and if you own a herding breed,
you can join in the activity.
Herding dogs are tested for
their natural skills to keep a
flock of ducks, sheep or cattle
together. If your dog shows
potential, you can start at the
testing level, where your dog can
earn a title for showing an inherent herding ability.
With training you can advance to the trial level, where
your dog should be capable of controlling even difficult livestock in diverse situations.

LURE COURSING

The AKC Tests and Trials for Lure Coursing are open
to traditional sighthounds—Greyhounds, Whippets,

Borzoi, Salukis, Afghan Hounds, Ibizan Hounds and Scottish Deerhounds—as well as to Basenjis and Rhodesian Ridgebacks. Hounds are judged on overall ability, follow, speed, agility and endurance. This is possibly the most exciting of the trials for spectators, because the speed and agility of the dogs is awesome to watch as they chase the lure (or "course") in heats of two or three dogs at a time.

TRACKING

Tracking is another activity in which almost any dog can compete because every dog that sniffs the ground when taken outdoors is, in fact, tracking. The hard part comes when the rules as to what, when and where the dog tracks are determined by a person, not the dog! Tracking tests cover a large area of fields, woods and roads. The tracks are laid hours before the dogs go to work on them, and include "tricks" like cross-tracks and sharp turns. If you're interested in search-and-rescue work, this is the place to start.

This tracking dog is hot on the trail.

EARTHDOG TESTS FOR SMALL TERRIERS AND DACHSHUNDS

These tests are open to Australian, Bedlington, Border, Cairn, Dandie Dinmont, Smooth and Wire Fox, Lakeland, Norfolk, Norwich, Scottish, Sealyham, Skye, Welsh and West Highland White Terriers as well as Dachshunds. The dogs need no prior training for this terrier sport. There is a qualifying test on the day of the event, so dog and handler learn the rules on the spot. These tests, or "digs," sometimes end with informal races in the late afternoon.

Here are some of the extracurricular obedience and racing activities that are not regulated by the AKC or UKC, but are generally run by clubs or a group of dog fanciers and are often open to all.

Canine Freestyle This activity is something new on the scene and is variously likened to dancing, dressage or ice skating. It is meant to show the athleticism of the dog, but also requires showmanship on the part of the dog's handler. If you and your dog like to ham it up for friends, you might want to look into freestyle.

Lure coursing lets sighthounds do what they do best—run!

Scent Hurdle Racing Scent hurdle racing is purely a fun activity sponsored by obedience clubs with members forming competing teams. The height of the hurdles is based on the size of the shortest dog on the team. On a signal, one team dog is released on each of two side-by-side courses and must clear every hurdle before picking up its own dumbbell from a platform and returning over the jumps to the handler. As each dog returns, the next on that team is sent. Of course, that is what the dogs are supposed to do. When the dogs improvise (going under or around the hurdles, stealing another dog's dumbbell, and so forth), it no doubt frustrates the handlers, but just adds to the fun for everyone else.

Flyball This type of racing is similar, but after negotiating the four hurdles, the dog comes to a flyball box, steps on a lever that releases a tennis ball into the air, catches the ball and returns over the hurdles to the starting point. This game also becomes extremely fun for spectators because the dogs sometimes cheat by catching a ball released by the dog in the next lane. Three titles can be earned—Flyball Dog (F.D.), Flyball Dog Excellent (F.D.X.) and Flyball Dog Champion (Fb.D.Ch.)—all awarded by the North American Flyball Association, Inc.

Dogsledding The name conjures up the Rocky Mountains or the frigid North, but you can find dogsled clubs in such unlikely spots as Maryland, North Carolina and Virginia! Dogsledding is primarily for the Nordic breeds such as the Alaskan Malamutes, Siberian Huskies and Samoyeds, but other breeds can try. There are some practical backyard applications to this sport, too. With parental supervision, almost any strong dog could pull a child's sled.

Coming over the A-frame on an agility course.

These are just some of the many recreational ways you can get to know and understand your multifaceted dog better and have fun doing it.

chapter 10

Your Dog
and your
Family

by Bardi McLennan

Adding a dog automatically increases your family by one, no matter whether you live alone in an apartment or are part of a mother, father and six kids household. The single-person family is fair game for numerous and varied canine misconceptions as to who is dog and who pays the bills, whereas a dog in a houseful of children will consider himself to be just one of the gang, littermates all. One dog and one child may give a dog reason to believe they are both kids or both dogs.

Either interpretation requires parental supervision and sometimes speedy intervention.

As soon as one paw goes through the door into your home, Rufus (or Rufina) has to make many adjustments to become a part of your family. Your job is to make him fit in as painlessly as possible. An older dog may have some frame of reference from past experience, but to a 10-week-old puppy, everything is brand new: people, furniture, stairs, when and where people eat, sleep or watch TV, his own place and everyone else's space, smells, sounds, outdoors—everything!

Puppies, and newly acquired dogs of any age, do not need what we think of as "freedom." If you leave a new dog or puppy loose in the house, you will almost certainly return to chaotic destruction and the dog will forever after equate your homecoming with a time of punishment to be dreaded. It is unfair to give your dog what amounts to "freedom to get into trouble." Instead, confine him to a crate for brief periods of your absence (up to three or four hours) and, for the long haul, a workday for example, confine him to one untrashable area with his own toys, a bowl of water and a radio left on (low) in another room.

Lots of pets get along with each other just fine.

For the first few days, when not confined, put Rufus on a long leash tied to your wrist or waist. This umbilical cord method enables the dog to learn all about you from your body language and voice, and to learn by his own actions which things in the house are NO! and which ones are rewarded by "Good dog." Housetraining will be easier with the pup always by your side. Speaking of which, accidents do happen. That goal of "completely housetrained" takes up to a year, or the length of time it takes the pup to mature.

The All-Adult Family

Most dogs in an adults-only household today are likely to be latchkey pets, with no one home all day but the dog. When you return after a tough day on the job, the dog can and should be your relaxation therapy. But going home can instead be a daily frustration.

Separation anxiety is a very common problem for the dog in a working household. It may begin with whines and barks of loneliness, but it will soon escalate into a frenzied destruction derby. That is why it is so important to set aside the time to teach a dog to relax when left alone in his confined area and to understand that he can trust you to return.

Let the dog get used to your work schedule in easy stages. Confine him to one room and go in and out of that room over and over again. Be casual about it. No physical, voice or eye contact. When the pup no longer even notices your comings and goings, leave the house for varying lengths of time, returning to stay home for a few minutes and gradually increasing the time away. This training can take days, but the dog is learning that you haven't left him forever and that he can trust you.

Any time you leave the dog, but especially during this training period, be casual about your departure. No anxiety-building fond farewells. Just "Bye" and go! Remember the "Good dog" when you return to find everything more or less as you left it.

If things are a mess (or even a disaster) when you return, greet the dog, take him outside to eliminate, and then put him in his crate while you clean up. Rant and rave in the shower! *Do not* punish the dog. You were not there when it happened, and the rule is: Only punish as you catch the dog in the act of wrongdoing. Obviously, it makes sense to get your latchkey puppy when you'll have a week or two to spend on these training essentials.

Family weekend activities should include Rufus whenever possible. Depending on the pup's age, now is the time for a long walk in the park, playtime in the backyard, a hike in the woods. Socializing is as important as health care, good food and physical exercise, so visiting Aunt Emma or Uncle Harry and the next-door neighbor's dog or cat is essential to developing an outgoing, friendly temperament in your pet.

If you are a single adult, socializing Rufus at home and away will prevent him from becoming overly protective of you (or just overly attached) and will also prevent such behavioral problems as dominance or fear of strangers.

Babies

Whether already here or on the way, babies figure larger than life in the eyes of a dog. If the dog is there first, let him in on all your baby preparations in the house. When baby arrives, let Rufus sniff any item of clothing that has been on the baby before Junior comes home. Then let Mom greet the dog first before introducing the new family member. Hold the baby down for the dog to see and sniff, but make sure some-

one's holding the dog on lead in case of any sudden moves. Don't play keep-away or tease the dog with the baby, which only invites undesirable jumping up.

The dog and the baby are "family," and for starters can be treated almost as equals. Things rapidly change, however, especially when baby takes to creeping around on all fours on the dog's turf or, better yet, has yummy pudding all over her face and hands! That's when a lot of things in the dog's and baby's lives become more separate than equal.

Dogs are perfect confidants.

Toddlers make terrible dog owners, but if you can't avoid the combination, use patient discipline (that is, positive teaching rather than punishment), and use time-outs before you run out of patience.

A dog and a baby (or toddler, or an assertive young child) should never be left alone together. Take the dog with you or confine him. With a baby or youngsters in the house, you'll have plenty of use for that wonderful canine safety device called a crate!

Young Children

Any dog in a house with kids will behave pretty much as the kids do, good or bad. But even good dogs and good children can get into trouble when play becomes rowdy and active.

Legs bobbing up and down, shrill voices screeching, a ball hurtling overhead, all add up to exuberant frustration for a dog who's just trying to be part of the gang. In a pack of puppies, any legs or toys being chased would be caught by a set of teeth, and all the pups involved would understand that is how the game is played. Kids do not understand this, nor do parents tolerate it. Bring Rufus indoors before you have reason to regret it. This is time-out, not a punishment.

Teach children how to play nicely with a puppy.

You can explain the situation to the children and tell them they must play quieter games until the puppy learns not to grab them with his mouth. Unfortunately, you can't explain it that easily to the dog. With adult supervision, they will learn how to play together.

Young children love to tease. Sticking their faces or wiggling their hands or fingers in the dog's face is teasing. To another person it might be just annoying, but it is threatening to a dog. There's another difference: We can make the child stop by an explanation, but the only way a dog can stop it is with a warning growl and then with teeth. Teasing is the major cause of children being bitten by their pets. Treat it seriously.

Older Children

The best age for a child to get a first dog is between the ages of 8 and 12. That's when kids are able to accept some real responsibility for their pet. Even so, take the child's vow of "I will never *ever* forget to feed (brush, walk, etc.) the dog" for what it's worth: a child's good intention at that moment. Most kids today have extra lessons, soccer practice, Little League, ballet, and so forth piled on top of school schedules. There will be many times when Mom will have to come to the dog's rescue. "I walked the dog for you so you can set the table for me" is one way to get around a missed appointment without laying on blame or guilt.

Kids in this age group make excellent obedience trainers because they are into the teaching/learning process themselves and they lack the self-consciousness of adults. Attending a dog show is something the whole family can enjoy, and watching Junior Showmanship may catch the eye of the kids. Older children can begin to get involved in many of the recreational activities that were reviewed in the previous chapter. Some of the agility obstacles, for example, can be set up in the backyard as a family project (with an adult making sure all the equipment is safe and secure for the dog).

Older kids are also beginning to look to the future, and may envision themselves as veterinarians or trainers or show dog handlers or writers of the next Lassie best-seller. Dogs are perfect confidants for these dreams. They won't tell a soul.

Other Pets

Introduce all pets tactfully. In a dog/cat situation, hold the dog, not the cat. Let two dogs meet on neutral turf—a stroll in the park or a walk down the street—with both on loose leads to permit all the normal canine ways of saying hello, including routine sniffing, circling, more sniffing, and so on. Small creatures such as hamsters, chinchillas or mice must be kept safe from their natural predators (dogs and cats).

Festive Family Occasions

Parties are great for people, but not necessarily for puppies. Until all the guests have arrived, put the dog in his crate or in a room where he won't be disturbed. A socialized dog can join the fun later as long as he's not underfoot, annoying guests or into the hors d'oeuvres.

There are a few dangers to consider, too. Doors opening and closing can allow a puppy to slip out unnoticed in the confusion, and you'll be organizing a search party instead of playing host or hostess. Party food and buffet service are not for dogs. Let Rufus party in his crate with a nice big dog biscuit.

At Christmas time, not only are tree decorations dangerous and breakable (and perhaps family heirlooms), but extreme caution should be taken with the lights, cords and outlets for the tree lights and any other festive lighting. Occasionally a dog lifts a leg, ignoring the fact that the tree is indoors. To avoid this, use a canine repellent, made for gardens, on the tree. Or keep him out of the tree room unless supervised. And whatever you do, *don't* invite trouble by hanging his toys on the tree!

Car Travel

Before you plan a vacation by car or RV with Rufus, be sure he enjoys car travel. Nothing spoils a holiday quicker than a carsick dog! Work within the dog's comfort level. Get in the car with the dog in his crate or attached to a canine car safety belt and just sit there until he relaxes. That's all. Next time, get in the car, turn on the engine and go nowhere. Just sit. When that is okay, turn on the engine and go around the block. Now you can go for a ride and include a stop where you get out, leaving the dog for a minute or two.

On a warm day, always park in the shade and leave windows open several inches. And return quickly. It only takes 10 minutes for a car to become an overheated steel death trap.

Motel or Pet Motel?

Not all motels or hotels accept pets, but you have a much better choice today than even a few years ago. To find a dog-friendly lodging, look at *On the Road Again With Man's Best Friend,* a series of directories that detail bed and breakfasts, inns, family resorts and other hotels/motels. Some places require a refundable deposit to cover any damage incurred by the dog. More B&Bs accept pets now, but some restrict the size.

If taking Rufus with you is not feasible, check out boarding kennels in your area. Your veterinarian may offer this service, or recommend a kennel or two he or she is familiar with. Go see the facilities for yourself, ask about exercise, diet, housing, and so on. Or, if you'd rather have Rufus stay home, look into bonded petsitters, many of whom will also bring in the mail and water your plants.

chapter 11

Your Dog
and your
Community

by Bardi McLennan

Step outside your home with your dog and you are no longer just family, you are both part of your community. This is when the phrase "responsible pet ownership" takes on serious implications. For starters, it means you pick up after your dog—not just occasionally, but every time your dog eliminates away from home. That means you have joined the Plastic Baggy Brigade! You always have plastic sandwich bags in your pocket and several in the car. It means you teach your kids how to use them, too. If you think this is "yucky," just imagine what the person (a non-doggy person) who inadvertently steps in the mess thinks!

Your responsibility extends to your neighbors: To their ears (no annoying barking); to their property (their garbage, their lawn, their flower beds, their cat—especially their cat); to their kids (on bikes, at play); to their kids' toys and sports equipment.

There are numerous dog-related laws, ranging from simple dog licensing and leash laws to those holding you liable for any physical injury or property damage done by your dog. These laws are in place to protect everyone in the community, including you and your dog. There are town ordinances and state laws which are by no means the same in all towns or all states. Ignorance of the law won't get you off the hook. The time to find out what the laws are where you live is now.

Be sure your dog's license is current. This is not just a good local ordinance, it can make the difference between finding your lost dog or not.

Dressing your dog up makes him appealing to strangers.

Many states now require proof of rabies vaccination and that the dog has been spayed or neutered before issuing a license. At the same time, keep up the dog's annual immunizations.

Never let your dog run loose in the neighborhood. This will not only keep you on the right side of the leash law, it's the outdoor version of the rule about not giving your dog "freedom to get into trouble."

Good Canine Citizen

Sometimes it's hard for a dog's owner to assess whether or not the dog is sufficiently socialized to be accepted by the community at large. Does Rufus or Rufina display good, controlled behavior in public? The AKC's Canine Good Citizen program is available through many dog organizations. If your dog passes the test, the title "CGC" is earned.

The overall purpose is to turn your dog into a good neighbor and to teach you about your responsibility to your community as a dog owner. Here are the ten things your dog must do willingly:

1. Allow a stranger to handle him or her as a groomer or veterinarian would.
2. Accept a stranger stopping to chat with you.
3. Walk nicely on a loose lead.
4. Walk calmly through a crowd.
5. Sit and be petted by a stranger.
6. Sit and down on command.
7. Stay put when you move away.
8. Casually greet another dog.
9. React confidently to distractions.
10. Accept being tied up in a strange place and left alone for a few minutes.

Schools and Dogs

Schools are getting involved with pet ownership on an educational level. It has been proven that children who are kind to animals are humane in their attitude toward other people as adults.

A dog is a child's best friend, and so children are often primary pet owners, if not the primary caregivers. Unfortunately, they are also the ones most often bitten by dogs. This occurs due to a lack of understanding that pets, no matter how sweet, cuddly and loving, are still animals. Schools, along with parents, dog clubs, dog fanciers and the AKC, are working to change all that with video programs for children not only in grade school, but in the nursery school and pre-kindergarten age group. Teaching youngsters how to be responsible dog owners is important community work. When your dog has a CGC, volunteer to take part in an educational classroom event put on by your dog club.

Boy Scout Merit Badge

A Merit Badge for Dog Care can be earned by any Boy Scout ages 11 to 18. The requirements are not easy, but amount to a complete course in responsible dog care and general ownership. Here are just a few of the things a Scout must do to earn that badge:

Point out ten parts of the dog using the correct names.

Give a report (signed by parent or guardian) on your care of the dog (feeding, food used, housing, exercising, grooming and bathing), plus what has been done to keep the dog healthy.

Explain the right way to obedience train a dog, and demonstrate three comments.

Several of the requirements have to do with health care, including first aid, handling a hurt dog, and the dangers of home treatment for a serious ailment.

The final requirement is to know the local laws and ordinances involving dogs.

There are similar programs for Girl Scouts and 4-H members.

Local Clubs

Local dog clubs are no longer in existence just to put on a yearly dog show. Today, they are apt to be the hub of the community's involvement with pets. Dog clubs conduct educational forums with big-name speakers, stage demonstrations of canine talent in a busy mall and take dogs of various breeds to schools for class-room discussion.

The quickest way to feel accepted as a member in a club is to volunteer your services! Offer to help with something—anything—and watch your popularity (and your interest) grow.

Therapy Dogs

Once your dog has earned that essential CGC and reliably demonstrates a steady, calm temperament, you could look into what therapy dogs are doing in your area.

Therapy dogs go with their owners to visit patients at hospitals or nursing homes, generally remaining on leash but able to coax a pat from a stiffened hand, a smile from a blank face, a few words from sealed lips or a hug from someone in need of love.

Nursing homes cover a wide range of patient care. Some specialize in care of the elderly, some in the treatment of specific illnesses, some in physical therapy. Children's facilities also welcome visits from trained therapy dogs for boosting morale in their pediatric patients. Hospice care for the terminally ill and the at-home care of AIDS patients are other areas where this canine visiting is desperately needed. Therapy dog training comes first.

Your dog can make a difference in lots of lives.

There is a lot more involved than just taking your nice friendly pooch to someone's bedside. Doing therapy dog work involves your own emotional stability as well as that of your dog. But once you have met all the requirements for this work, making the rounds once a week or once a month with your therapy dog is possibly the most rewarding of all community activities.

Disaster Aid

This community service is definitely not for everyone, partly because it is time-consuming. The initial training is rigorous, and there can be no let-up in the continuing workouts, because members are on call 24 hours a day to go wherever they are needed at a moment's notice. But if you think you would like to be able to assist in a disaster, look into search-and-rescue work. The network of search-and-rescue volunteers is worldwide, and all members of the American Rescue Dog Association (ARDA) who are qualified to do this work are volunteers who train and maintain their own dogs.

Physical Aid

Most people are familiar with Seeing Eye dogs, which serve as blind people's eyes, but not with all the other work that dogs are trained to do to assist the disabled. Dogs are also specially trained to pull wheelchairs, carry school books, pick up dropped objects, open and close doors. Some also are ears for the deaf. All these assistance-trained dogs, by the way, are allowed anywhere "No Pet" signs exist (as are therapy dogs when

Making the rounds with your therapy dog can be very rewarding.

properly identified). Getting started in any of this fascinating work requires a background in dog training and canine behavior, but there are also volunteer jobs ranging from answering the phone to cleaning out kennels to providing a foster home for a puppy. You have only to ask.

part four

Beyond the Basics

chapter 12

Recommended Reading

Books

ABOUT HEALTH CARE

Ackerman, Lowell. *Guide to Skin and Haircoat Problems in Dogs.* Loveland, Colo.: Alpine Publications, 1994.

Alderton, David. *The Dog Care Manual.* Hauppauge, N.Y.: Barron's Educational Series, Inc., 1986.

American Kennel Club. *American Kennel Club Dog Care and Training.* New York: Howell Book House, 1991.

Bamberger, Michelle, DVM. *Help! The Quick Guide to First Aid for Your Dog.* New York: Howell Book House, 1995.

Carlson, Delbert, DVM, and James Giffin, MD. *Dog Owner's Home Veterinary Handbook.* New York: Howell Book House, 1992.

DeBitetto, James, DVM, and Sarah Hodgson. *You & Your Puppy.* New York: Howell Book House, 1995.

Humphries, Jim, DVM. *Dr. Jim's Animal Clinic for Dogs.* New York: Howell Book House, 1994.

McGinnis, Terri. *The Well Dog Book.* New York: Random House, 1991.

Pitcairn, Richard and Susan. *Natural Health for Dogs.* Emmaus, Pa.: Rodale Press, 1982.

ABOUT DOG SHOWS

Hall, Lynn. *Dog Showing for Beginners.* New York: Howell Book House, 1994.

Nichols, Virginia Tuck. *How to Show Your Own Dog.* Neptune, N. J.: TFH, 1970.

Vanacore, Connie. *Dog Showing, An Owner's Guide.* New York: Howell Book House, 1990.

ABOUT TRAINING

Ammen, Amy. *Training in No Time*. New York: Howell Book House, 1995.

Baer, Ted. *Communicating With Your Dog*. Hauppauge, N.Y.: Barron's Educational Series, Inc., 1989.

Benjamin, Carol Lea. *Dog Problems*. New York: Howell Book House, 1989.

Benjamin, Carol Lea. *Dog Training for Kids*. New York: Howell Book House, 1988.

Benjamin, Carol Lea. *Mother Knows Best*. New York: Howell Book House, 1985.

Benjamin, Carol Lea. *Surviving Your Dog's Adolescence*. New York: Howell Book House, 1993.

Bohnenkamp, Gwen. *Manners for the Modern Dog*. San Francisco: Perfect Paws, 1990.

Dibra, Bashkim. *Dog Training by Bash*. New York: Dell, 1992.

Dunbar, Ian, PhD, MRCVS. *Dr. Dunbar's Good Little Dog Book*, James & Kenneth Publishers, 2140 Shattuck Ave. #2406, Berkeley, Calif. 94704. (510) 658–8588. Order from the publisher.

Dunbar, Ian, PhD, MRCVS. *How to Teach a New Dog Old Tricks*, James & Kenneth Publishers. Order from the publisher; address above.

Dunbar, Ian, PhD, MRCVS, and Gwen Bohnenkamp. Booklets on *Preventing Aggression; Housetraining; Chewing; Digging; Barking; Socialization; Fearfulness; and Fighting*, James & Kenneth Publishers. Order from the publisher; address above.

Evans, Job Michael. *People, Pooches and Problems*. New York: Howell Book House, 1991.

Kilcommons, Brian and Sarah Wilson. *Good Owners, Great Dogs*. New York: Warner Books, 1992.

McMains, Joel M. *Dog Logic—Companion Obedience*. New York: Howell Book House, 1992.

Rutherford, Clarice and David H. Neil, MRCVS. *How to Raise a Puppy You Can Live With*. Loveland, Colo.: Alpine Publications, 1982.

Volhard, Jack and Melissa Bartlett. *What All Good Dogs Should Know: The Sensible Way to Train*. New York: Howell Book House, 1991.

ABOUT BREEDING

Harris, Beth J. Finder. *Breeding a Litter, The Complete Book of Prenatal and Postnatal Care*. New York: Howell Book House, 1983.

Holst, Phyllis, DVM. *Canine Reproduction*. Loveland, Colo.: Alpine Publications, 1985.

Walkowicz, Chris and Bonnie Wilcox, DVM. *Successful Dog Breeding, The Complete Handbook of Canine Midwifery*. New York: Howell Book House, 1994.

ABOUT ACTIVITIES

American Rescue Dog Association. *Search and Rescue Dogs*. New York: Howell Book House, 1991.

Barwig, Susan and Stewart Hilliard. *Schutzhund*. New York: Howell Book House, 1991.

Beaman, Arthur S. *Lure Coursing*. New York: Howell Book House, 1994.

Daniels, Julie. *Enjoying Dog Agility—From Backyard to Competition*. New York: Doral Publishing, 1990.

Davis, Kathy Diamond. *Therapy Dogs*. New York: Howell Book House, 1992.

Gallup, Davis Anne. *Running With Man's Best Friend*. Loveland, Colo.: Alpine Publications, 1986.

Habgood, Dawn and Robert. *On the Road Again With Man's Best Friend*. New England, Mid-Atlantic, West Coast and Southeast editions. Selective guides to area bed and breakfasts, inns, hotels and resorts that welcome guests and their dogs. New York: Howell Book House, 1995.

Holland, Vergil S. *Herding Dogs*. New York: Howell Book House, 1994.

LaBelle, Charlene G. *Backpacking With Your Dog*. Loveland, Colo.: Alpine Publications, 1993.

Simmons-Moake, Jane. *Agility Training, The Fun Sport for All Dogs*. New York: Howell Book House, 1991.

Spencer, James B. *Hup! Training Flushing Spaniels the American Way*. New York: Howell Book House, 1992.

Spencer, James B. *Point! Training the All-Seasons Birddog*. New York: Howell Book House, 1995.

Tarrant, Bill. *Training the Hunting Retriever*. New York: Howell Book House, 1991.

Volhard, Jack and Wendy. *The Canine Good Citizen*. New York: Howell Book House, 1994.

General Titles

Haggerty, Captain Arthur J. *How to Get Your Pet Into Show Business*. New York: Howell Book House, 1994.

McLennan, Bardi. *Dogs and Kids, Parenting Tips*. New York: Howell Book House, 1993.

Moran, Patti J. *Pet Sitting for Profit, A Complete Manual for Professional Success*. New York: Howell Book House, 1992.

Scalisi, Danny and Libby Moses. *When Rover Just Won't Do, Over 2,000 Suggestions for Naming Your Dog.* New York: Howell Book House, 1993.

Sife, Wallace, PhD. *The Loss of a Pet.* New York: Howell Book House, 1993.

Wrede, Barbara J. *Civilizing Your Puppy.* Hauppauge, N.Y.: Barron's Educational Series, 1992.

Magazines

The AKC GAZETTE, The Official Journal for the Sport of Purebred Dogs. American Kennel Club, 51 Madison Ave., New York, NY.

Bloodlines Journal. United Kennel Club, 100 E. Kilgore Rd., Kalamazoo, MI.

Dog Fancy. Fancy Publications, 3 Burroughs, Irvine, CA 92718

Dog World. Maclean Hunter Publishing Corp., 29 N. Wacker Dr., Chicago, IL 60606.

Videos

"SIRIUS Puppy Training," by Ian Dunbar, PhD, MRCVS. James & Kenneth Publishers, 2140 Shattuck Ave. #2406, Berkeley, CA 94704. Order from the publisher.

"Training the Companion Dog," from Dr. Dunbar's British TV Series, James & Kenneth Publishers. (See address above).

The American Kennel Club produces videos on every breed of dog, as well as on hunting tests, field trials and other areas of interest to purebred dog owners. For more information, write to AKC/Video Fulfillment, 5580 Centerview Dr., Suite 200, Raleigh, NC 27606.

chapter 13

Resources

Breed Clubs

Every breed recognized by the American Kennel Club has a national (parent) club. National clubs are a great source of information on your breed. You can get the name of the secretary of the club by contacting:

The American Kennel Club
51 Madison Avenue
New York, NY 10010
(212) 696-8200

There are also numerous all-breed, individual breed, obedience, hunting and other special-interest dog clubs across the country. The American Kennel Club can provide you with a geographical list of clubs to find ones in your area. Contact them at the above address.

Registry Organizations

Registry organizations register purebred dogs. The American Kennel Club is the oldest and largest in this country, and currently recognizes over 130 breeds. The United Kennel Club registers some breeds the AKC doesn't (including the American Pit Bull Terrier and the Miniature Fox Terrier) as well as many of the same breeds. The others included here are for your reference; the AKC can provide you with a list of foreign registries.

American Kennel Club
51 Madison Avenue
New York, NY 10010

United Kennel Club (UKC)
100 E. Kilgore Road
Kalamazoo, MI 49001-5598

American Dog Breeders Assn.
P.O. Box 1771
Salt Lake City, UT 84110
(Registers American Pit Bull Terriers)

Canadian Kennel Club
89 Skyway Avenue
Etobicoke, Ontario
Canada M9W 6R4

National Stock Dog Registry
P.O. Box 402
Butler, IN 46721
(Registers working stock dogs)

Orthopedic Foundation for Animals (OFA)
2300 E. Nifong Blvd.
Columbia, MO 65201-3856
(Hip registry)

Activity Clubs

Write to these organizations for information on the activities they sponsor.

American Kennel Club
51 Madison Avenue
New York, NY 10010
(Conformation Shows, Obedience Trials, Field Trials and Hunting Tests, Agility, Canine Good

Citizen, Lure Coursing, Herding, Tracking,
Earthdog Tests, Coonhunting.)

United Kennel Club
100 E. Kilgore Road
Kalamazoo, MI 49001-5598
(Conformation Shows, Obedience Trials, Agility,
Hunting for Various Breeds, Terrier Trials and
more.)

North American Flyball Assn.
1342 Jeff St.
Ypsilanti, MI 48198

International Sled Dog Racing Assn.
P.O. Box 446
Norman, ID 83848-0446

North American Working Dog Assn., Inc.
Southeast Kreisgruppe
P.O. Box 833
Brunswick, GA 31521

Trainers

Association of Pet Dog Trainers
P.O. Box 3734
Salinas, CA 93912
(408) 663–9257

American Dog Trainers' Network
161 West 4th St.
New York, NY 10014
(212) 727–7257

**National Association of Dog Obedience
Instructors**
2286 East Steel Rd.
St. Johns, MI 48879

Associations

American Dog Owners Assn.
1654 Columbia Tpk.
Castleton, NY 12033
(Combats anti-dog legislation)

Delta Society
P.O. Box 1080
Renton, WA 98057-1080
(Promotes the human/animal bond through
pet-assisted therapy and other programs)

Dog Writers Assn. of America (DWAA)
Sally Cooper, Secy.
222 Woodchuck Ln.
Harwinton, CT 06791

National Assn. for Search and Rescue (NASAR)
P.O. Box 3709
Fairfax, VA 22038

Therapy Dogs International
1536 Morris Place
Hillside, NJ 07205